D1135142

Our Debt to Greece and Rome

EDITORS

GEORGE DEPUE HADZSITS, PH.D.

DAVID MOORE ROBINSON, PH.D., LL.D.

ALFRED EDWARD TAYLOR, British Philosopher educated at New College, Oxford, received the degrees of D.Litt. and LL.D. He was Professor of Moral Philosophy at St. Andrews and Edinburgh for thirty-three years. Among his works are *Aristotle on His Predecessors, St. Thomas Aquinas as a Philosopher, Plato, the Man and His Work* and *The Life of Socrates.*

PORTRAIT OF PLATO
Discovered recently at Holkham Hall, England.
Reproduced from *Journal of Hellenic Studies*, XL (1920),
pl. VIII.

PLATONISM
AND ITS INFLUENCE

BY
ALFRED EDWARD TAYLOR
PROFESSOR OF MORAL PHILOSOPHY

COOPER SQUARE PUBLISHERS, INC.
NEW YORK
1963

41796

Published 1963 by Cooper Square Publishers, Inc.
59 Fourth Avenue, New York 3, N. Y.
Library of Congress Catalog Card No. 63-10308

To
MY WIFE
A. E. T.

DILIGITE JUSTITIAM QUI IUDICATIS TERRAM

CONTENTS

CHAPTER   PAGE

       PREFACE ix

  I. THE PLATONIC TRADITION 3

 II. THE PRINCIPLES OF SCIENCE . . . 29

III. THE RULE OF LIFE 57

IV. PLATO THE THEOLOGIAN 97

       NOTES 135

       BIBLIOGRAPHY 146

PREFACE

THE writer's object in the following pages has deliberately been not so much to supply information as to provoke the desire for it. If any of his readers should be led by anything he has said to seek further knowledge of Plato and his influence on thought and literature, in the works mentioned in the appended *Bibliography* or in other places, the end will have been attained.

With regard to the many disputed questions connected with the interpretation of Plato, the writer has done his best to be silent where he could, and where he could not, to indicate his own opinions, without assuming that they are necessarily the true ones because they are his. Ample divergence of views will be found even within the limits of the few works named in the *Bibliography*.

PLATONISM
AND ITS INFLUENCE

PLATONISM AND ITS INFLUENCE

I. THE PLATONIC TRADITION

TO few men does the world owe a heavier debt than to Plato. He has taught us that "philosophy," loving and single-minded devotion to truth, is the great gift of God to man and the rightful guide of man's life, and that the few to whom the intimate vision of truth has been granted are false to their calling unless they bear fruit in unwearied and humble service to their fellows. All worthy civilization is fed by these ideas, and whenever, after a time of confusion and forgetfulness, our Western world has recaptured the sense of noble living it has sought them afresh in the Platonic writings. Plato has been called, with some truth, the father of all heresies in religion and science; he has been, in the same degree, a fountain of all that

[3]

is most living in all the orthodoxies. Not, to be sure, that philosophy sprang full grown from the soul of Plato, like Athena from the brain of Zeus. No man simply discovers truth whole and entire by his unaided genius. The great thinkers know better than any of us the flippant error suggested by such a line as " God said, Let *Newton* be, and all was light." Plato is never weary of hinting that he is the spiritual heir of two earlier great men, Socrates and Pythagoras. But, as neither of these great men wrote anything, it is chiefly through Plato that they have influenced all later ages and are a living force in the thought of today. Pythagoras still influences us chiefly through the *Phaedo* and *Philebus* and *Timaeus,* and without Plato's dialogues Socrates would be to us little more than *magni nominis umbra.* So also, when we speak of the historical influence of Plato, we must not forget our debt to his great disciple, Aristotle. But Aristotle owes the best of his inspiration to influences received from personal contact with Plato, and it is the Platonic strain in his thinking which has appealed most strongly to later ages. That " domination of the human mind by the authority of Aristotle " which popular imagination strangely exaggerates is itself an episode in the fortunes of Platonism.

Plato's thought had not to be learned by his associates and immediate successors, as it must be by ourselves, primarily from his writings. These, as their style shows, were addressed to the educated public at large. Many of the most finished of them (*Protagoras, Gorgias, Symposium, Phaedo,* probably most of the *Republic*) were composed before the writer had found his real vocation as the president of a permanently organized society for the pursuit of " research." Even those which are certainly subsequent to the founding of the Academy (*Theaetetus, Parmenides, Sophistes, Politicus, Timaeus, Philebus, Laws*), seem to be meant in the main to give the world at large some notion of the studies and methods of Plato's school. To Plato's own mind the organized inquiries of the school itself were his principal " work." This is why even the latest dialogues make no explicit mention of the things which Aristotle specifies as most distinctive of Platonism, and why Aristotle can assume that the audience at his lectures on *Ethics,* whose interests would be those of the practical statesman rather than those of

[5]

the speculative philosopher, will know the text of the *Philebus* and *Laws* as a seventeenth century Puritan knew King James's Bible.

Plato had, indeed, no high opinion of mere reading as an incentive to thinking, and on that ground refused to compile a *Treatise* of his own philosophy.[1] For philosophy and science are not collections of statements which can be written down and conned; they are the actual life of a mind engaged in the quest for truth. The fire must be alight in a man's own soul; all that one man can do for another is to convey the spark which kindles it, and that only in the intimacy of a shared daily life and shared pursuits. As a living religion presupposes a Church, so a living science presupposes organized co-operation in " research." This is why we can form no adequate conception of Platonism by merely reading the dialogues without actual knowledge of the achievement of Plato's Academy in mathematical, physical and moral science. The school, we must remember, had an unbroken corporate existence from its foundation (c. 387 B.C.) down to the suppression of its organization and the embezzlement of its endowments by Justinian (529 A.D.), a longer life than has yet

[6]

been enjoyed by any modern University. This explains why the literary works of Plato, unlike those of Democritus or Aristotle, have not perished, and why the text of our best Plato manuscripts is so exceptionally good. But if Aristotle and his contemporaries could base their most important statements about Plato's doctrines directly on their own recollection of his personal teaching, subsequent generations were necessarily dependent on the dialogues, supplemented by the exegetical traditions of the early Academy and such express references to the " unwritten doctrines " as could be found in Aristotle and his contemporaries. Cicero was in this respect in much the same position as ourselves.

From the first there were divergencies of exegesis within the Academy on difficult points. Xenocrates, the second successor of Plato, a contemporary of Aristotle, discussed the meaning of the account of the " birth of the soul " in the *Timaeus,* and Crantor, the most eminent Academic of the third generation, wrote an elaborate *Memoir* on the subject. Crantor's interpretation diverged from that of Xenocrates, and Aristotle's differs still more widely from both. From the time of Arcesilaus, fifth president of the school (d. 241 B.C.), to that of Carneades (d. 129 B.C.), the Academy was chiefly busied with a destructive criticism of the dogmatic sensationalism of the Stoics. Hence we get the tradition, as old as the first century B.C., that Arcesilaus and his followers (the so-called "New" Academy) were mere sceptics, "academics" in the sense in which Hume adopted the name. This cannot well be the unqualified truth. When a genuinely sceptical school arose in the opening centuries of our era, its members made a strong point of refusing to admit the scepticism of the Academy. It is also certain that all through the first and second centuries A.D., there was a strong current of popular Platonism which preserved the main positive doctrines of Plato though with modifications in an Aristotelian sense. We see this from the so-called *Timaeus Locrus*, the recently discovered fragmentary commentary on the *Theaetetus*, the long passages preserved by Eusebius from the second-century Platonist Atticus, the *Introduction to Platonism* by Alcinous, the essays of Plutarch and the discourses of Maximus of Tyre, all works from this period. It is very hard to understand the persistence of this tradition and the familiarity of a man like Plutarch with the Platonic exegesis of Xenocrates and Crantor if we believe the Academy to have become a home of scepticism by 250 B.C. The real facts are perhaps disclosed by Cicero's *Academica*. Early in the first century B.C., there was a deliberate attempt to read Stoicism bodily into Plato, just as eminent Stoics of the same period, Panaetius and Posidonius, were trying to read Plato into Stoicism. Antiochus of Ascalon declared that Plato and Socrates had taught the same doctrine as Zeno, the founder of Stoicism, though in different language, and that the polemic of Arcesilaus was therefore a departure from the true spirit of the Academy. The actual head of the Academy, Philo of Larissa, replied by denying that there had ever been any real change in the school's doctrine.[2] Cicero tells us that the controversy caused a great sensation.

Since Plato always denied the possibility of founding science on sense-perception alone, Philo was clearly right and Antiochus wrong on the main issue; presumably Philo was equally right in denying that there had ever been any material change in the Academic teaching. The assertions of Antiochus are only a mark of the same eclectic spirit of the times which was equally shown in the Platonizing of Stoicism by Panaetius and Posidonius. It is probable enough that Arcesilaus and his successors no longer devoted themselves, like the earlier Academics, to mathematics and physical science, but that is a mere consequence of the severance between " philosophy " and " positive science " effected in the third century B.C. For good or ill the rise of the great Alexandrian institutes for the prosecution of the sciences in independence of the philosophical schools divorced philosophy from mathematics and cosmology and made the reduction of metaphysics to mere " epistemology " inevitable.[3]

The actual history of the Academy after the time of Philo and Antiochus is obscure. But we have plentiful material on which to base a knowledge of the generally diffused popular Platonism of the first two Christian centuries. To the works already mentioned we may add the voluminous writings of the famous Philo of Alexandria, in which the Old Testament Scriptures are allegorized by the help of a highly Stoicized Platonism. The most striking feature of this popularized Platonism is its combination of Plato's doctrine about God and the " intelligible Forms " with the Aristotelian conception of an eternal " formless " matter as the substratum upon which God impresses, or from which He educes, the various " forms " of things. The ethical side of the doctrine is the theory, entirely foreign to Plato, of " matter " as the cause of evil. Plutarch and Atticus professed to find this " formless matter " in the *Timaeus,* in defiance of the older Academic exegesis of the dialogue.

The ultimate revival of the full philosophy of Plato, with its further elaboration as an intellectual basis for Hellenism in its struggle with the rising Christian Church, took place independently of the official Academy, not at Athens but at Rome. It was the work of Plotinus, the last man of first-rate genius among the Greek philosophers. Of his origin we know nothing, and of his early life no more than that he pursued his studies at Alexandria. His school was opened at Rome, where, according to his biographer, Porphyry, he had settled in the first year of the Emperor Philip (245 A.D.), and it is important to observe that neither Alexandria nor Athens played any important part in the school's history. His philosophy,

in fact, only captured the Academy in the fifth
century, and this want of connection with
Plato's original foundation probably explains
why Plotinus and his followers always called
themselves simply " Platonists," never " Academics." Plotinus and his successors believed
that they were, in all matters of principle, reviving the genuine thought of Plato, and the
belief may be allowed if we add that the Plato
of Plotinus is inevitably Plato seen through a
temperament. The Neo-Platonic interpretation of Plato is dominated by the passion for
a fully articulated vision of the world as a
structural unity. In Plato's own writings there
is an imperfectly filled gap between the doctrine of the Forms, the basis of the Platonic
theory of science, and the doctrine of God and
the soul which is the foundation of his theory
of nature and human life. Plotinus tries to
bridge the gap, relying mainly on the great
passage of the *Republic* about that ineffable
Good which is at once the source of all things
and itself " on the further side of Being." [3]
He and his followers elaborated the famous
conception of the scale, or ladder, of successive " emanations " or " progressions " which
connect this supreme Good with the whole

hierarchy of its increasingly blurred and imperfect "images." Wherever in later philosophy or theology we come upon the "scale of
being" or "ladder of perfection" we may be
sure that we are dealing with the influence of
Plato transmitted through Plotinus.

In two respects the effects of this revival
were curiously unlike anything which its authors can have intended. Plotinus pursues the
task of philosophic construction in a spirit of
all but complete detachment from the heats
of controversy, but among his immediate followers the polemic against the aspirations of
the nascent Catholic Church to replace philosophy as the guide of life came into prominence.
Porphyry was the founder of Biblical "higher
criticism," and the relentless destruction of his
work *Against the Christians* shows how damag-
ing his attack was felt to be. In the fourth
century, the "Platonists" formed the nucleus
of the last opposition to the triumph of the
Church; it was from them that the Emperor
Julian selected his coadjutors in his ill-judged
scheme of reaction. Proclus, the great sys-
tematizer of the school, was living (410–485
A.D.) in an age when Christianity was firmly
established as the official faith, and had to

content himself with the practice of a fanciful Pagan " Catholicism," and the occasional enlivenment of his lectures by a few harmless sarcasms. As a private " fad " the rejection of Christianity even survived the closing of the school by Justinian. But the positive work of the Neo-Platonists was completed by Proclus. His successors had, for the most part, to content themselves with preserving in erudite commentaries the scientific tradition of a past which the barbarian invasions were already threatening to engulf. The active continuance of speculation had already passed into the hands of Christian divines. The real importance of Proclus in history is that he, more than any one, provided theologians with an intellectual framework for their view of the world and Christian mystics with a reasoned defence of the " way of negation."

So also the later Platonists unwittingly paved the way for the future " domination of Aristotle," a domination of which there had as yet been, and for centuries to come would not be any trace. The genuine Hellenic tradition had never been in the least dominated by Aristotle. His doctrine as a self-subsistent philosophy can hardly be said to have outlived his successor,

Theophrastus (d. 288 B.C.). Down to at least
150 A.D., so far as there is a living alternative
to Platonism among serious thinkers, it is
Stoicism. As is well known, Cicero never
treats any third choice as possible, though in
certain moods he wonders whether, after all,
Stoicism may not be the only genuine philosophy. Aristotle he regards as, for all serious
purposes, only Plato over again. The revival of
Aristotelian studies to which we owe the commentaries of Alexander of Aphrodisias (end
of second century A.D.) makes no difference
in the general situation; from Theophrastus to
Plotinus the philosophers who really " count "
are always either Platonists or Stoics, though,
naturally, traces of Aristotelian ideas are to be
found in both successions. The leading names
in mathematics and science are usually those
of men who belong to no philosophical school.
In particular, it is a mistake to attribute the
long reign of the " Ptolemaic " astronomy to
any philosophical bias. Its true authors, Hipparchus and Ptolemy, were mathematicians,
not philosophers, and the theory, which agrees
with Aristotle's own only in being geocentric,
was adopted precisely because Aristotle's machinery of concentric " spheres " was found to

be irreconcilable with the results of careful observation. Throughout the Alexandrian and Roman periods, so far as astronomy, biology, medicine are influenced by any philosophical classic, the dominant influence is, as it continued to be throughout most of the Middle Ages, that of the *Timaeus*.

The first step to the canonization of Aristotle as an authority in science was taken in the school of Plotinus. His works were read there as well as those of Plato, and his logical treatises were looked on as a necessary preliminary to the study of Plato's metaphysics and theology. Porphyry's *Introduction* to Aristotelian logic thus became the source of the great mediaeval controversies about "universals." When, with the triumph of Christianity, the school was driven more and more to busy itself with harmless erudition, it was natural that the erudition should be displayed in the exegesis of Aristotle's monographs on the various sciences. Hence the last valuable productions of the school are to be found in the minute and learned commentaries of Simplicius on Aristotle's physical, cosmological and psychological writings. Little as men like Simplicius intended the result, the pains they lavished on this work probably did more than any other single cause to make Aristotle, read with their comments, the master of encyclopaedic knowledge in the eyes of mediaeval Jews, Arabs and Christians.

Meanwhile, before the time of Proclus the Christian Church had become the real heir of Platonic philosophy. Even before the time of Plotinus, she was already appealing to Plato as an ally in her controversy with the " Gentiles." Clement of Alexandria — to mention only the most prominent name — at the opening of the third century, in his *Protrepticus,* confounds idolatry and immoral mythology by the conjunct authority of the Hebrew prophets and of Plato, whom he regards as having the same sort of mission to the Greeks as Jeremiah or Ezekiel to Israel. In his *Miscellanies* he constantly goes to Plato as well as to Scripture for the foundation of what he intends to be a distinctively Christian philosophy. The lengths to which Origen went, in the next generation, in reading the eschatology of Plato's myths into Christianity, are notorious. His theories were finally repudiated by the Church, but the tendency of which they are the outcome was continued in the fourth century by the Cappadocian divines, notably by St. Gregory of Nyssa, from whom the Platonic influence passed to the West through St. Ambrose of Milan, still within the fourth century. Five hundred years later, Gregory's ideas were to be reproduced with startling effect by Joannes Scotus Erigena.

It was by a different route that Platonism found its way into the main current of Western orthodoxy. This is principally the work of two great men, St. Augustine and Boethius. Augustine, the greatest figure of the Western Church and the author of what is most distinctive in its theology, had been deeply influenced, before his conversion, by the study of Plotinus in a Latin version. In a famous passage of his *Confessions*, he says that the only fundamental truth that he had not found in the "Platonists" was the doctrine of the Incarnation.[4] Boethius furnished the West with its knowledge of logical doctrine by his expositions of Porphyry and Aristotle, and with its standard formula of orthodoxy by his tracts on the doctrines of the Trinity and the Person of Christ. What was even more important, in the imprisonment which preceded his death, he wrote a small volume which remained all through the

Middle Ages the most popular of all serious books, the *Consolatio Philosophiae*. Here the Platonic cosmology and natural theology is expounded with singular charm and grace as a basis for the justification of God's mysterious ways with man. Since Boethius had given the standard formulation of the two chief doctrines of the Church and had met his death at the hands of the Arian Theodoric (525 A.D.), he was popularly looked on as a saint and martyr, and this reputation enhanced the influence of the exquisite book which reclaimed Dante from an unworthy life and counts King Alfred and Chaucer among its English translators.[5]

A secondary potent source of Platonism in mediaeval thought and literature are the writings of the so-called "Dionysius the Areopagite," which laid the foundations of mediaeval angelology and the mediaeval theory of mysticism. These works are, in fact, only a superficially Christianized version of Proclus, but were readily accepted in the Dark Age as the authentic compositions of an immediate disciple of St. Paul, and supposed to embody a revelation made to the Apostle when he was "caught up to the third heaven." They were made accessible to the West in the ninth century by the Latin version of Scotus Erigena and continued to exercise enormous influence until their authenticity was questioned by the Humanists of the fifteenth century; but even later, their attraction continued.[6]

The channels through which Platonism passed into the thought of the Western Church are, in the main, these three, Augustine, Boethius, Dionysius, and the Plato who thus influenced theology is primarily Plato seen through the medium of Plotinus. Scientific thought in the Middle Ages was also influenced by Plato in another way. The West possessed all along the philosophical works of Cicero, and what was more important, the fifth-century commentary of Macrobius on Cicero's *Somnium Scipionis*. Most important of all, it had the fourth-century Latin translation by Chalcidius of the first two-thirds of the *Timaeus* with his Commentary on the text. Thus, until the translation of Aristotle's metaphysical and scientific works from the oriental versions into Latin began, the West had really much more adequate information about Plato, especially about the *Timaeus,* than about Aristotle. The *Timaeus* was, in fact, the only

really great Greek philosophical work accessible to the West in the early Middle Ages.
Accordingly we find that down to the beginning of the thirteenth century, the dominant
position of Plato and Augustine remains un-
shaken, though in the twelfth century the influence of Aristotelian logic makes itself
powerfully felt in such writers as Abelard and
Hugh of St. Victor, and, in particular, gives rise
to the acrimonious controversy about the nature of " universals." But it is still Augustine
who reigns in theology and the *Timaeus* which
dictates the conception of the physical world
found in the encyclopaedias of writers like
Honorius of Autun.

The discovery of Aristotle as something
more than a formal logician and his elevation
to the rank of supreme authority in science
belong to the thirteenth century, the golden
age of scholasticism. The versions of Aristotle known to the twelfth century, coming
through the hands of Neo-Platonizing Arabs,
Moors and Jews, offer a text in which Aristotle
himself is largely Platonized; with the next
century the West gradually acquires new
translations, made directly from the Greek,
in which the philosopher's metaphysical and

physical teaching is presented free from Neo-Platonic accretions.[7] The Church was naturally at first suspicious of a new knowledge coming through the hands of heretics and " miscreants," and more than once the teachers of the new university of Paris, which Innocent III and his successors hoped to make the great centre for the training of a learned priesthood, were interdicted from lecturing in public on any works of Aristotle other than the familiar logical treatises. The change by which, before the end of the century, Aristotle came to be recognized as the highest authority in all branches of natural knowledge was directly due to the genius and industry of two Dominicans, Albert the Great and St. Thomas Aquinas. The revolution was not effected without great searchings of heart, nor was it everywhere successful. Its real character is often misunderstood. To us the work of Albert and Thomas might seem to amount to an enslavement of the human intellect; to themselves, as Professor Étienne Gilson rightly insists, it must have appeared as a great enfranchisement. Albert and Thomas, with the aid of Aristotle, had, in fact, rediscovered nature as an object of study in its own right and not a mere collection of symbols embodying theological truths. St. Thomas' introduction of a hard and fast distinction between reason and revelation in effect gave the mind a *Magna Charta* which set it free henceforth to study everything that falls outside the narrow circle of revealed dogma, in complete indifference to theological *arrière-pensées*. Hence Professor Gilson has called St. Thomas the first " modern " philosopher and remarked that the revolution made by him and his teacher Albert is the one example in all Church history of a " modernist " movement that has succeeded.[8]

The triumph of Thomas does not mean that the Platonic-Augustinian tradition was simply broken off short. St. Bonaventura, in whom mediaeval Augustinianism reaches its fullest development, is a contemporary and friend of Thomas. In England, where Thomism never really became at home, the Augustinian tradition, combined with the spirit of devotion to mathematical and experimental science, was ardently cultivated all through the century by the Franciscans of Oxford, Robert Grosseteste, Roger Bacon and their friends.[9] We have probably to thank the independent attitude of the University of Oxford for the very preservation to Europe of mathematics and physical science during the critical time while the re-sounding success of St. Thomas was turning the minds of the ablest men in the University of Paris to the employment of philosophy in the construction of natural theology and the refutation of the " infidel."

In the next century there is an important reaction of Oxford on Paris and indirectly on Europe at large. There is still a popular fiction that the discrediting of Aristotle's kinematics — necessary for the foundation of a really scientific mechanics — was achieved by Galileo single-handed, or only with the assistance of Kepler, at the reopening of the seventeenth century. But, in fact, the Aris-totelian errors had been detected and consider-able advance made towards a sounder theory in the fourteenth century by such men as John Buridan, Nicholas of Autrecour, Albert of Sax-ony, whose philosophical inspiration came from the famous Oxonian, William of Ockham. The violent opposition offered to Galileo by the Italian Universities was the death struggle of a doctrine which had been already tried and found wanting north of the Alps.[10] In France, too, Descartes by no means stood alone in his revolt against the " schools." The revival of Augustinianism was a feature both of the social circle to which he belonged and of the Jesuit teaching on which he had been brought up at La Flèche.[11] In the case of both Galileo and Descartes emancipation from Aristotelianism led to a conception of scientific method and an appreciation of the importance of mathematics which is characteristically Platonic.

If this little book were concerned with the influence of Plato on general literature, much would have to be said of the effect of the revival of Greek in the fifteenth and sixteenth centuries in creating an enthusiasm for the greatest of all Greek writers. One would have to speak of the half-fantastic " Academy " of Lorenzo dei Medici and of the scholars who composed it, and again of the half-scientific, half-poetic " emancipated spirits " of the late sixteenth century, Bruno and Campanella, and of the Platonic studies of members of noble English families who had come under Italian influences. Here it must be sufficient to note that this widely diffused familiarity with Plato on his imaginative side explains the frequent echoes of him which pervade Elizabethan and Jacobean literature. Marlowe and Shakespeare break into language which reveals close familiarity with the whole Pythagorean-Platonic mythology of the soul on the slightest provocation. The ease and naturalness with which Shakespeare moves in this circle of ideas is a reasonable proof that he was neither Bacon nor any other " man of learning." His knowledge sits far too lightly to have been won by burning the midnight oil. Bacon himself knows his Plato, and in him, as in other anti-Aristotelians, revulsion from Aristotelian dogma is accompanied by admiration for the more flexible thought of Plato. So the Augustinian influence shows itself strongly in the first great English divine after the Reformation, Hooker. It is even more marked in the next century, in the whole group of " Cambridge " divines, Cudworth, More and their friends, who vindicated spiritual religion in the very unspiritual age of Charles II. We might fairly say that Plato and Augustine have been the intellectual sources of Anglican theology at its best, from Hooker to Westcott, and Platonic conceptions the founda-

tion of the ethics of the greatest men of the
classical period of British moral philosophy,
Cudworth, Butler, Richard Price, John Grote.

In a different way Platonic conceptions
have re-emerged at the critical points in the
history of modern science. When Leibniz and
Newton founded the Calculus in the seventeenth century, they were going back to mathematical ideas which had originated in the first
generation of the Academy, and the predecessors upon whom they were directly building,
Cavalieri, Wallis, Barrow, were men who had
taken up geometry precisely where the Academy had left off. Perhaps we might add that
the further work of Weierstrass and his followers who have, within our own lifetime, made
the Calculus a strictly logical development
from the first principles of the science of number, has been the execution of a task clearly
indicated by Plato, though insoluble without
the help of methods which did not exist in his
own day. In the most recent attempt to con-
struct an adequate Philosophy of Nature, Dr.
Whitehead has found himself led to take as
his starting point the general view of nature
put by Plato into the mouth of Timaeus.[12] It
certainly looks as if the *Timaeus* may once

again come to be the standing background for the educated man's vision of Nature.

This chapter has attempted to indicate in a general way the line of descent by which Platonic ideas have become part of the unconscious inheritance of the educated man of to-day, and the times at which their influence has received a new accession of strength. Incidently we have seen that the supposed " age-long " subjugation of the human mind by Aristotle is little more than a myth. The subjugation does not really begin until after the middle of the thirteenth century and its spell is already pretty thoroughly broken by the end of the fourteenth. Even if we allow for the general persistence of the intellectual habit long after the most original minds have shaken themselves free from it, it is worth while to remember that Dante (1265– 1321) is the first unqualified Aristotelian among the great names of European literature, although he too was captivated by Boethius, while the whole paraphernalia of scholastic Aristotelianism are a mere jest to Rabelais (d. 1553).

II. THE PRINCIPLES OF SCIENCE

THE leading ideas of Plato's theory of the nature and objects of scientific knowledge can be stated very simply. Thinking is not the same thing as the having of sensations; it is not literally true that " seeing is believing." All thinking is *judgment* and needs to be expressed in *propositions,* and no proposition is the mere record of the occurrence of a sensation. With Plato, as with Kant, the distinction between thought and sensation is fundamental. He neither, like the Associationists, regards thinking as a kind of attenuated " sensation," nor, with Leibniz, treats sensation as a kind of confused thinking. This is one reason why Plato, like Kant, is accused by his opponents of dividing the universe into " two worlds."

Again, not all thinking is knowledge or science. We have to distinguish what we really know from what we merely think or believe. For (1) we are perfectly sure of what we know and we can say exactly what it is; when we only think or believe, we are not sure, and we often are unable to formulate our belief with any precision. (2) If a man really knows a proposition, he can "give and receive argument" about it; he can produce rational grounds for his conviction of its truth. This cannot be done when you merely think or believe. (3) Knowledge can be communicated only by the production of good and sufficient grounds, but you can get men to share a mere belief, as skilled advocates in the Law Courts or on the political platform habitually do, by appeals to their emotions or prejudices.[13]

The distinction just drawn is to be understood in an ontological and not in a merely psychological sense. It answers to a real difference of character between *objects* of which it is possible to have knowledge and those about which we can at best have opinions or beliefs. If the truths of science are certain, definite and apprehended with intellectual necessity, the objects known must have a character which is unvarying, completely determinate and wholly luminous to the intellect. Science must thus be concerned with what is eternal, definite and through and through intelligible, and with nothing else. Typical

[30]

examples of a realm of such objects are yielded by mathematics and again by ethics. Triangles or circles and their properties are the same independently of all variations of place and date; their characters are wholly determinate, and determined by conditions of which the geometer is completely aware. Plato holds that the same is true of the objects of the moralist's study, good, right, the virtues. But if there are objects which are always " in the making " and never fully made, whose very " being " is change or development, their characters will be fluid, changing with place and date, and our statements about them will always be liable to revision; in such statements there will always be an extra-rational element of mere given " brute " fact. This distinction between what is eternal, fully determinate and wholly intelligible, and what is temporal, fluid and weighted with an element of inexplicable " fact," is precisely the distinction between a realm where we are dependent wholly on thinking and a realm in which we have to take the reports of our senses about the occurrence of something at a given place and time as data for our thinking. It is only when the data of our

thinking contain no such elements, that thinking leads to the results with the character
Plato demands of everything that can be called
science. Knowledge is attained only by the
activity of " the mind by herself, apart from
the instruments of sense-perception," [14] and
this is the historical reason why we still continue to speak of " pure " mathematics or
" pure " ethics. Where the mind is dependent
on the " instruments of sense " we have only
beliefs or judgments which Plato will not dig-
nify with the name of knowledge. The distinction thus corresponds fairly with that
drawn by some modern thinkers between the
" timeless " realm of ideals or values and the
" temporal " realm of " actual " facts.[15] But
Plato is convinced that only what can stand
the most rigid scrutiny of the intellect really
is. Hence he calls the " ideals " of pure thinking " what is," and speaks of the " actual "
and " sensible " as something " which never is
but is always becoming." [16] The whole of
what we call " nature," or " the sequence of
events," the system of interconnected facts revealed by our senses, is thus, on Plato's view,
outside the range of knowledge proper; it is
only by a loose use of language that we give

the name " science " to our convictions about it. Strictly speaking, what the " natural " sciences have to tell us is no more than " likely stories."

This does not mean that we are not to pursue the " natural " sciences, or that any one " story " about such matters is as likely as another. If nature is always " in the making," our stories about it can only be provisional, and can never have the finality of mathematics or ethics, but that is no reason why we should not aim at coming as near to finality as we can. The more we look for definite order and law in the sensible world, the more we shall find of it, though we shall never wholly get rid of the element of brute fact for which no reason can be assigned except that " you see it happens so." Our " stories " will always be provisional, subject to revision as our stock of " facts " grows, but, for that very reason, they will always be " progressive." If the element of unaccountable brute " fact " in nature cannot be completely eliminated, we can at least set ourselves to diminish it without limit, and it is just in this that the true work of " physical science " lies.[17]

These are the thoughts which lie at the

bottom of what has commonly been called the
" Platonic theory of Ideas." The name is
better avoided because in English the word
" idea " conveys associations which are quite
misleading. The *ideai*, " figures," " patterns,"
" forms " of which we read in Plato are in no
sense " states " or " processes " of our minds,
nor is their existence supposed to depend on
the existence of any mind whatever. The
Forms are just those absolutely determinate
objects of thinking which, in Plato's language,
" are " and do not " become," and which it is
the business of science to know completely.
We may, if we like, call them " concepts," provided that we remember two things: (1) they
are that which is known, not the act or process
of knowing it; (2) their existence does not depend on that of a mind which " conceives "
them; minds know them but do not make
them. More exactly, we might say that a
Form is that which is *denoted* by a significant
universal term. Such examples as " the number 2 " in arithmetic, " the regular pentagon "
in geometry, " the exactly right act " in morals,
will illustrate for us what is meant. No Form
is apprehended by sense-perception. We never
see a " perfect circle " or two absolutely equal

[34]

lengths; we do not meet with absolute and perfect moral goodness in the life of any man of flesh and blood.[18] Yet the world of pure thought and that of the senses are not simply disconnected. We do see figures which approximate in different degrees to circularity, and we meet some men who are nearer moral perfection than others. In such cases, we know what it is that is being approximated to, we know that it is only approximated to, not reached, and, often at least, we can say which of two figures or of two men, approximates more nearly to circularity or to goodness. Plato expresses this by saying that sensible things " partake of " or " participate in " Forms, and again by saying that the Form is a " model " of which the sensible thing is a " copy " or " imitation." Aristotle tells us that the second of the formulae, that of " imitation," was originally Pythagorean. Plato himself indicates that the metaphor of " participation " comes from Socrates.[19] It is important to remember that, as there is nothing sensible which does not " participate " in a Form or Forms, so there is no Form which is not " participated " in by something sensible.

The proper object of knowledge is always

a Form. Yet it is certain that when we begin our life on earth as babies we do not bring ready-made knowledge of the Forms with us. Plato knows nothing of such a crude doctrine of " innate ideas " as is often erroneously imputed to Descartes. Our earthly life begins with sensations which the baby does not know how to interpret.[20] How do we advance to the apprehension of the Forms? How, in fact, do we learn to know? In the *Phaedo* Socrates says that though sense-experience does not directly exhibit the Forms, it *suggests* them to us. If I see the portrait of an absent friend or some article belonging to him, I am not seeing my friend, but what I do see " reminds me " of him, suggests the thought of him. So I never see a perfectly straight line, but the sight of sticks which are more or less crooked suggests the thought of the perfect straightness which I do not see. Sense-experience exhibits a series of more remote or closer approximations to an " ideal limit," and so suggests the ideal limit itself. This is what is really meant by the doctrine that all learning is " being reminded " of something. The standing Platonic illustration of this is that by drawing a suitable figure and asking the right questions you can get a lad to see for himself the truth of a geometrical proposition which he has never been " taught." [21]   The point is that though sensation does not directly reveal scientific truths, as the empiricists suppose, it is always pregnant with them.   The truths have to be discovered by an effort of thinking, but sense-experience starts the effort by suggesting to a mind which can think, as well as feel, truths which it does not disclose.   The all-important point for our purpose is that this theory of the suggestiveness of sensation implies a view of thought quite inconsistent with the restriction of its function to the mere work of " abstraction."   " Abstraction," if you use the word with accuracy, means separating from a number of experiences the features which are common to them all, and neglecting those which are only present in some of them.   But when the sight of a number of rods " suggests " to me a perfect straightness which I admit not to have been exhibited by any one of them, that which is suggested is precisely what was *not* there in any of the suggesting experiences, and, *a fortiori, not* there in all of them.

The theory of scientific method characteristic of Plato is what we should expect in one who held the theory of the object of science just explained. Socrates puts the matter very simply in the *Phaedo*.[22] In studying any problem, he says, his method is to begin by considering the " hypothesis " which appears to be the best available and asking what " consequences " would follow from this " hypothesis." If the " consequences " turn out not to be in accord with fact, the " hypothesis " is discredited. If they are " verified," the " hypothesis " is *so far* confirmed. But if its truth is still disputed the problem now becomes that of showing that the initial " hypothesis " itself can be deduced as a " consequence " from some more ultimate " hypothesis " which is not disputed. This process has to be repeated until we reach an " hypothesis " on which all parties to the inquiry are in agreement. By an " hypothesis," in this statement, is meant not a tentative guess, but, as we should say, a " postulate." There is no question of *demonstrating* an " hypothesis." If it is challenged, it must be shown to be a logical " consequence " of some other " hypothesis " which is not challenged, and the end of such a process would only be reached when the whole chain of deductions had been traced back to a principle for which immediate self-evidence could be claimed.

In the *Republic* [23] a rather fuller account of the matter is given. It is noted as a defect of the sciences, as commonly pursued, that each of them starts with a number of initial " hypotheses " or assumptions, which are never allowed to be criticized and yet are not really self-evident. Dialectic, or as we should say, Metaphysics, will therefore make the examination of these assumptions its object. It will, in fact, aim at " destroying the hypotheses," that is, at abolishing their supposed ultimate character, by getting behind them to principles which are really self-luminous. It will then descend again from these principles, when it has discovered them, and exhibit the unproved postulates of the various sciences as so many consequences of them. The ideal is something like such a reduction of the exact sciences to the status of deductions from a few ultimate principles as is attempted in the *Principia Mathematica* of Whitehead and Russell, with the difference that Plato expects the ultimate principles, when reached, to exhibit direct self-evidence.

What we know of the mathematical work of

the Academy shows that the method of the *Phaedo* was actually followed in its researches. In principle the method is that known to the ancient geometers as " analysis," the method of finding the proof of a theorem or the construction of a problem by first supposing the required proof or construction to have been completed and then reasoning backwards to find the conditions of solution. If the conditions, when found, include nothing but theorems or constructions of which we are already in possession, the problem is solved. The tradition which represents the method of analysis as actually discovered for the first time by Plato can hardly be correct; but it points to the habitual and characteristic use of the method in the early Academy.[24] Similarly in astronomy, the first systematic theory of the planetary motions, that of Eudoxus, is known to have been offered as the solution of a " problem " propounded to the school by Plato, " by the assumption of what and how many uniform motions may the appearances in the heavens be saved? " That is, — what is the simplest combination of regular movements into which we can analyze the observed data so as to do adequate justice to them all? (To " save the appearances " is the Academic formula for what we call the empirical verification of a scientific theory.) Manifestly this theory of the objects and methods of science has been primarily inspired by reflection on mathematics, the one branch of knowledge which had attained by Plato's time what Kant calls *den sicheren Gang der Wissenschaft*. Plato's own representation is that the conception of Forms as the proper objects of knowledge and the distinction between them and " what becomes " are due to the mathematical philosophers of the Pythagorean Order. The recognition of ethical Forms and the conception of sensible things as " participating " in the Forms he seems to ascribe to Socrates.[25] In the ideal of the systematic unification of all knowledge by a derivation of all special " postulates " from one set of self-luminous truths we may perhaps see a further development due to Plato himself.

The main doctrine, then, may be stated thus. Sense and thought are radically disparate, yet everywhere connected. Nature, the realm revealed by our senses, is only half-real, but it suggests a further reality which lies beyond itself. It is a system of symbols, and we ascend to truth by learning to pass from the symbols to the non-sensuous realities symbolized. (Christian thought was dominated by this view of nature from St. Augustine to St. Thomas, and it has never really outgrown it.)

But the Augustinian doctrine derives directly from Plato as seen through the temperament of Plotinus. What Nature symbolizes is now taken to be the God who is declared to be the source both of Nature and of the Forms she half-discloses. This God is also the author of Scripture. The doctrine now works out thus. The one absolutely real Being is God Himself, who, in fact, *is* Being. All other beings, just because they are not self-subsistent, only " partake " of Being. They also have limitations, and thus partake of " non-being," or are only partially real. [So also, God is the only completely adequate object of knowledge. True knowledge must always be knowledge of an object which really and wholly *is;* so far as there is an element of unreality in anything, that thing cannot be known in the full sense of the word, for the imperfectly real must also be the imperfectly knowable. [In the words of St. Hilary, *Perfecta scientia Deum scire.*

Hence, full and adequate knowledge, being knowledge of God Himself, is only possible to God. To know God completely as he is, *per essentiam suam,* is impossible to a creature, because the understanding of a creature is itself created, and therefore "partakes of" non-being.[26] God, then, can be known, even by the most exalted creature, only through inadequate manifestations of Himself. Man, having fallen through sin, is peculiarly faulty in deciphering the symbolism through which God reveals himself. In the case of man, this symbolism is double. God reveals Himself still, as he did at first to Adam, through the symbolism of Nature, but since Adam's sin we have become myopic in our vision. In His mercy, God also reveals Himself through an infallible Scripture of which the Church is the custodian. But in Scripture God is revealed, in a way adapted to our imperfect and now clouded intelligence, by metaphors and analogies drawn from the creatures, as a cloud, a fire, a lion, a lamb, an eagle, a worm, and in many other figures. The interpretation of these conflicting metaphors would be hopeless, were it not that the two symbolisms, the natural and the scriptural, having the same God for their source and their object, must be concordant.

Thus Nature, rightly understood, becomes a key to the divine hieroglyphics of Scripture. This is the only reason why Nature has an interest for the mind. In its own right Nature would not concern the intellect at all, for the proper and adequate object of the intellect is not the symbols but the God whom they partially disclose. *Fecisti nos ad Te, et inquietum est cor nostrum donec in Te requiescat.* The Christian begins by an act of simple faith. He accepts the Scriptural revelation as officially propounded by the Church, as infallible, but as yet he does not know what the infallible truth contained in Scripture is. This is the proverbial *foi de charbonnier,* and it suffices for salvation. But it is our natural desire and our duty, so far as we can, to go on to understand what we believe, and here the knowledge of Nature's symbols comes to our aid. We know that God is, in Scripture, called " light "; the better we understand the part played by light in the economy of the sensible world, the better we shall understand what this language is meant to teach us about

[44]

God.⟩ God calls Himself a "lion"; to know what this means we go to the Bestiaries for their lore about the lion and his ways. The true reason for seeking information about Nature is that given by St. Paul, that the invisible things of God have been made known from the beginning by the things which are visible.[27]

On this view, there is no real distinction between religion and philosophy, since philosophy is simply the use of our intelligence in deciphering Scripture by the aid of Nature. So too, before the time of Albert and Thomas, no sharp distinction was made between truths about God which can be discovered by "natural reason" and those which can only be made known by revelation. St. Anselm tries to prove the Trinity and the Incarnation by "reason"; St. Thomas teaches that they can only be known by revelation. But this does not mean that Anselm is more "rationalistic," in the modern sense of the word, than Thomas. It means that Anselm has no clear conception of any thing that we should call "natural" knowledge, as no one could have who held to the view that only God is wholly real and only the wholly real a proper object of knowledge. Anselm's "rationalism" is also a complete "supernaturalism"; it arises from sheer inability to think of Nature itself as a field for genuine knowledge.

The Augustinian view of the relation of God to the creation is clearly based in the end on the Platonic contrast between that which "is" and that which "becomes." So the central doctrine of the Augustinian theory of knowledge is Platonic in origin. It too starts from the radical disparity of sense and thought and the conception of sense-experience as serving to suggest something which it does not contain. The task of knowledge is to recover, — as Plato says, to "recollect" — the lineaments of the non-sensible reality from the hints and suggestions of its sensible shadow. To the Christian mind this means to discover the Creator behind his handiwork. The mystery, to be sure, is that the things of sense should have any suggestiveness for us, that they should be, as Berkeley was to put it, the vocables for "divine language." [28] How comes the human mind to be accessible to suggestion?

In outline, the Augustinian answer is that the human intellect is from the first illumined by the action of the Creator. God, who is "light" and the "father of lights," acts as the *lumen intellectus.* Plato had made Socrates say that the supreme Form, " the Good," is the source not only of all we know, but of our knowledge of itself and all other Forms, as the sun is at once the fountain of life and of the light by which we see itself and all it shines on.[28a] The Christianized version of this is the doctrine that God, the source of the light by which we see Him in His revealed word, is equally the source of the light by which we are awakened to the suggestiveness of natural things. Nature and Scripture alike are read by aid of this direct light from God. There is thus no difference in principle between natural knowledge and the divine knowledge which makes wise unto salvation. All knowledge is, indeed, revelation, though revelation has a double form, revelation through Nature and revelation in Scripture. This is why all the Augustinians, from Augustine to Bonaventura, say that Christ, the Word of the Father, is *magister ad omnia,* our teacher in secular learning no less than in divine.

The view of knowledge elaborated in the thirteenth century by Albert and Thomas stands in direct opposition to this Christianized Platonism. Thomas fastens on just that side of Aristotle's complex and doubtfully coherent theory of knowledge which stands in sharp opposition to Platonism. The doctrine, as he understands it, dispenses with the thought of sensation as suggestive of what it is powerless to reveal. The work of the intellect in constructing science consists simply in educing and disentangling from sensuous experiences what is implicitly contained in them; the one function of thought is thus to abstract and generalize, by attending to the common elements of a group of sense-experiences. The "universals" are thought of not as beyond the things apprehended by sense, but as contained in them and calling merely for disentanglement. With this reduction of thought to the capacity for abstraction and generalization goes the introduction of a sharp distinction between the "natural light" necessary for secular science and the supernatural light by which God is made known in revelation. Nature is thought of no longer as a "divine language" but simply as the handiwork of an artificer. Instead of a direct message from God in Nature, we are told that we must only expect to find few and faint traces of the craftsman in his handiwork. The earlier view had been that the world is a mirror where, in spite of its flaws, we can still discern the reflected features of God. On the later view it is only an effect from which we have to infer, if we can, the nature of its concealed cause. Hence the distress felt by many devout souls upon the promulgation of a doctrine which seemed to remove a supposedly present God to an inaccessible distance. Hence also the sharp Thomistic distinction between the doctrines of " natural " theology, which can be demonstrated by the unaided reason, and the specific dogmas of Christianity, which are indemonstrable and have to be accepted on the strength of a particular revelation. Hence, too, the persistency of Thomist thinkers in our own time in opposition to all *a-priorism* in the theory of knowledge, and the sympathy they show with empiricists whose metaphysical conclusions are commonly so different from their own. Plato and Kant, the two philosophers who most emphatically assert the total disparity of sense and thought, are also the two whom Thomists appear to find it hardest to understand or criticize with any sympathy.

We have already seen that the Thomistic reaction against the Platonic-Augustinian tradition was in part an important advance. With Thomas and his teacher, Albert, the conception of " natural *science* " definitely stamped itself on the thought of Western Europe, never to be forgotten again. The two things we miss in the Thomistic conception of this science are (1) the Platonic conviction that the basis of any satisfactory physical science must be sought in mathematics, and (2) the Platonic sense of the *provisionality* of all results attained in physical science and the consequent necessity of systematic and accurately registered experimentation if we are to be duly acquainted with the " appearances " to be " saved " by scientific theory. Both points are duly kept in the forefront by Roger Bacon and the Franciscans of Oxford, where Thomism never displaced the traditional Christianized Platonism. It is said, in particular, that we owe the very expression *scientia experimentalis* to Roger Bacon, the biggest figure of the Oxford group.

In later times the influence of Plato and Augustine has always made itself felt in the reactions which have followed the periods when philosophy has been dominated by empiricist views about knowledge. It would not be true to call the doctrine either of Aristotle or of Thomas empiricist without a great deal of qualification. But it is true that Thomism agrees with empiricism in rejecting the *a priori* in all its forms. All our knowledge, apart from that which rests on a specific revelation, is regarded as elaborated out of sensible data by abstraction and generalization. Even in the matter of religion, the tendency of Thomism, on the whole, is to disregard the possibility of those vague and confused but impressive immediate " contacts " with the divine on which Augustinianism lays stress, and to reduce " saving faith " as much as possible to an intellectual acquiescence in authoritative dogmatic formulae.[29] It leaves little room for anything like the " inner light."

The next great constructive philosophy, that of Descartes, reverts to something much more like the Platonic position. In the doctrine of innate ideas Descartes is half reviving the Platonic view of sense as suggestive of what it does not contain, in conscious opposition to the Thomist restriction of the function of thought to abstraction and generalization of what is already implicitly contained in sense. When Descartes maintains that our " clear and distinct ideas," notably the idea of God, are *innate,* his meaning is that by reflection on our scientific knowledge we may discover that it implies these conceptions, and that they are manifestly not derived from sense-experience by any process of abstraction. Sense-experience may furnish us with the occasion for the reflection, but the " ideas " themselves, since they transcend all sense-experience, cannot have been extracted from it. It is strictly in order that Descartes should have revived the Platonic reverence for mathematics as the most obvious example of a knowledge wholly intellectual and *a priori,* and the Platonic demand that natural science should be based on mathematics, since it is just our possession of mathematical concepts presupposing the process of " passing to a limit " which is the great stumbling block for all mere empiricism, as Hume has proved so elaborately. So it is part of the same recoil from Thomism that Descartes agrees with Anselm and the Augustinians after Anselm that the " ontological proof " of God's existence, the contention that we have only to understand what is meant by " the perfect being " to see that the existence of this being is self-evident, is valid. It is not surprising to

learn that Descartes' immediate circle consisted largely of men who were interested in
reviving Augustinian ideas in divinity in
opposition to unqualified Thomism, or that
Malebranche, the most illustrious figure of the
Cartesian succession, definitely returns to the
pre-Thomistic theory of knowledge and out-
does it by his own doctrine that all knowledge
is a direct illumination of the mind by immediate contact with God, in whom we contem-
plate the " intelligible " ideas of things.
Malebranche's *a-priorism* is thus much more
extreme than Plato's. Sensation, with him,
has no cognitive value at all, not even that of
suggestiveness. It is a mere physical " occasion " for the illuminative action of God on
the mind. Malebranche should, in fact, have
regarded the very existence of bodies as a
gigantic hallucination, (as Berkeley sometimes
does) but for his assumption that their reality
is guaranteed by Scriptural revelation.[30]

A still more illustrious example of the persistence of the Platonic tradition is furnished
by Leibniz. When Leibniz corrects the Thomist formula *nihil est in intellectu quod non
prius fuerit in sensu* by the famous addition
nisi intellectus ipse, he really means to be re-

viving the concept of the "suggestiveness" of sense against the reduction of the *intellectus possibilis* to a mere capacity for "abstraction." He too provides us with a more than Platonic *a-priorism*.[31] In his scheme each "monad" is a little world in itself and there is no real physical interconnection between one monad and another. Each develops from within, but the lines of development of all are so adjusted that there is an appearance of complete interconnection, just as a choir of musicians, each rendering his own score correctly, could keep time and tune, though no one of them might be aware of the existence of the rest. Strictly speaking, it follows that none of us ever knows anything but himself and his own "inner states"; of the rest of the world he only knows its reflection in himself. Thus all sensation, as well as all thought, comes to be strictly *a priori*. It is only by an inconsistency that Leibniz escapes an atheistic solipsism. This is the price philosophy has to pay when it substitutes for the Platonic disparity of sense and thought the conception of sensation as "confused thinking." Of the echo of the Platonic-Augustinian tradition in Berkeley's conception of nature as a divine language by

[54]

which God holds direct intercourse with his rational creatures something has already been said.

The most Platonic strain in the whole of eighteenth century philosophy, so far as the theory of knowledge is concerned, however, is the revival independently by Kant and by Reid of the doctrine of the radical disparity of sense and thought. It is unnecessary to dwell here on the fundamental importance of this doctrine for the *Critique of Pure Reason;* unfortunately Reid is less studied than he deserves to be, and this makes it worth while to remark that the same distinction is equally fundamental for his annihilating examination of the presentationism of Hume. Reid and Kant between them may be said to have delivered sane philosophy once more from the two rival errors which had beset it since the time of Descartes, the *a-priorist* error of treating perception as a kind of confused thinking and the sensualist error of regarding thinking as a pale and shadowy revival of sense-perception. In Kant's case the reversion to the Platonic position would appear to be unconscious; the frequent references to Plato, especially to the *Theaetetus,* in Reid suggest that with him the

[55]

dependence on Plato is direct and conscious.[32] It is not too much to say that, after more than two thousand years, the ultimate issues in "epistemology" are still those which are expounded with unequalled simplicity in the *Theaetetus,* the best general introduction to the problem of knowledge ever composed. Of the marked Platonic influence on the ethical thought of the classic British moralists, itself, in fact, part of the persistent Augustinianism of divinity in England, something will have to be said in another connection.

We have already called attention to the way in which first the invention of the Calculus and then the "arithmetization" of mathematics, so characteristic of the last half-century, are the realization of a Platonic ideal.[33] At the present moment it looks as though we were on the eve of an equally significant development in the philosophy of Nature which will take us back again to the doctrines of the *Timaeus,* with its distinction between "being" and "passage" or "becoming," and its theory of the limits of rational explanation in science as the starting point for a right understanding of the general task of physics and chemistry.[34]

III. THE RULE OF LIFE

PLATONIC influence on all our thinking about the practical conduct of life has been and still is incalculable. In this realm empiricism has always shown itself peculiarly superficial, while Aristotelianism has, in the main, repeated Plato's doctrine a little coarsened and with a certain diminution of moral fervour. If we sometimes underestimate our debt in these matters to Plato, it is only because Platonic ideas have become so completely part and parcel of our best tradition in morals and religion. His influence, like the pressure of the atmosphere, goes undetected because we never really get free from it.

In Plato's own mind, the whole doctrine of the right direction of human conduct is a unity, and it is only for reasons of convenience that we can draw distinctions between his ethical, political and religious teaching. Here he is followed in part by Aristotle, and still more by the great Christian moralists. None of them ever dream of divorcing Politics from

Ethics, or doubt that the principles of right action are the same for individuals and for social groups. Aristotle's personal tastes and peculiar circumstances, indeed, led him to cut his theology dangerously loose from his ethics, but the influence of the Scriptures has always prevented his Christian followers from surrendering themselves too completely to this tendency. Their divinity has always been more Platonic than their metaphysics.

Plato's moral doctrine has a healthy wholeness of outlook; it keeps consistently together points of view which have often been separated, but always with disastrous effects. He, like the empiricists, holds that the one reasonable aim of action is " happiness " or " felicity," but he knows human nature too well to look for felicity in excitement or in the " maximum of agreeable feeling." His sense of the unconditional obligatoriness of right action is as keen as Butler's or Kant's, but he is free from the perverted psychology which led Kant to think it wrong to do the most harmless act for the sake of " human pleasure," and almost to hold that the virtuous act is only truly virtuous when done " against the grain." Like Aristotle and Spinoza, he holds that the right is also the reasonable and that our unreason is the source of our misdoing, but his sense of the reality of sin saves him from the moral shallowness too often found in " rationalistic " Ethics. His sense of sin is as genuine as Pascal's or Kant's, but it never leads him, as it led those great moralists, into a virtual Manichaeism. Like the mystics, he is keenly alive to the distinction between " eternal " and " temporal " good, yet he never forgets that, if " detachment " is necessary to noble living, the true detachment is that of the man who uses temporal good without losing his heart to it. Hence he never forgets the real importance of temporal problems, from that of governing a State to that of seeing that a baby gets the right kind of food and the right kind of play.

Roughly stated, the main thought of Platonic Ethics is this. Man's life is a perpetual search for something he has not got, though without it he can never be at peace with himself. This something is " the good for man," " that which would make any man's life happy," [35] if only he had the fruition of it. If most men live and die without knowing what true happiness is, the reason is not that they do not desire it — at heart they never desire anything else — but that they look for it in the wrong place. They confuse it with the round of pleasures, with health and long life, with worldly wealth, or with that irresponsible power which, by lifting its possessor above all law enables him always to "do as he likes." But satisfaction is not to be found in any of these things. The pursuit of pleasures is self-defeating, and those who get most of them find that in the end they bring very little of what they promised; "excitement" really has more of the bitter in it than of the sweet.[36] It is not the having of strength, long life, health, wealth, but the right use of them which makes a man happy. "Doing what you like" is the most wretched life of all; it is because the "autocrat, who is above all law," always does as he likes that he never gets what all men's hearts are set upon.[37] The ultimate source of human unhappiness is thus not "unpropitious circumstance" but the inner division of the soul, the conflict of "passion," which prompts us always to do as we like, with judgment, which bids us aim at true felicity. No one would ever choose anything *because* he saw that it was bad for him; we choose what is bad for us, and so are unhappy, because we mistake it for good. Sin is thus the real cause of misery, and the source of sin is ignorance or error, the mistaking of evil for good. Hence the need of " philosophy " for the direction of life; the whole object of philosophy is to lead us into a sure and abiding knowledge of good and evil, and so to make our judgment and the conduct which ensues from it, sound, and to restore the soul to health and unity with itself. Philosophy is, as Socrates had called it, the art of the " tendance of the soul," and the chief reason for prizing even the most " abstract " science is not that it amuses our curiosity, but that it is a discipline in thinking which makes us fit to judge rightly of good and evil.

Philosophy, then, delivers us from sin by delivering us from false judgment and guiding us to a true estimate of the various kinds of good. There are three main kinds, goods of fortune, goods of the body, goods of the soul. Philosophy teaches us that a man's soul is the most precious thing about him, because it is most peculiarly himself; the body, again, is more truly myself than any of my belongings. Hence the rule of right judgment is that the best of all goods is goodness of soul, virtue and wisdom; goodness of body comes only second, and the "goods of fortune" third. A sound judgment will always prefer virtue to health or strength and these to mere wealth or rank or power. Indeed, exceptionally lusty strength is, in various ways, unfavourable to virtue, and great affluence to both virtue and bodily health, and a right-judging man would not wish to have either the physique of Heracles or the wealth of a Croesus or Callias. The one brings with it gross lusts and intellectual dullness, the other pride and wantonness and softness.[38] But Plato is no enemy of human pleasure. He is fully prepared to argue the point that, even by the rules of the calculus of pleasure and pain, if you formulate the rules correctly and work the sum right, the life of the man who puts the soul first, the body second and "fortune" only third, will prove to be the most truly agreeable as well as the most noble. He is at special pains to establish this result because, as he says, it is not gods but men whom we want to enlist on the side of right living, and so we must make allowance for the universal human desire for pleasurable existence.[39]

We may state the same view of human felicity rather differently in the way familiar to readers of the *Republic*. There is a hierarchy of what Butler would call "principles of action" in each of us. There are first a host of appetitions for particular gratifications; we may group them all under the general name of "concupiscence," and say that the man who is dominated by them lives for "the body," because these gratifications are of a sensual kind, or for "pleasure," or for "wealth," because what he cares for is the command of the satisfactions which can be bought and sold. Next there is an element of "spirit," chivalrous emotion, which shows itself alike in tenacity of our rights, in justified or unjustified ambition and in the scorn of self which we feel when we have yielded to what we regard as unworthy cravings. The man in whose life this factor is dominant may be said to be aiming at "distinction"; at his best, he furnishes us with our honourable soldiers and sportsmen; at his worst, he is the aspiring "careerist." Finally there is the principle of judgment and there are the men who govern their lives by adherence to a consistent judgment of good and evil, the "philosophers." If a man is to be at peace with himself, there must be a right relation between these three principles of action, and the one right relation is that true judgment of good and bad should dictate the law of our life, that our "point of honour" should lie in loyal adhesion to its dictates, and that "concupiscence" should be confined within the limits prescribed by judgment and honour. Departure from this rule of life is sin; the greater the departure, the graver the sin, the deeper the misery resulting from the division within the self.

No man is born with this disciplined order ready-made in him; we have all to be schooled into it and restrained from violating it. This is the real reason why the State, with its rules and organization, is necessary to man. The State's supreme function is education, the training of noble personality. If we are to achieve such personality, our discipline must begin in our earliest days and must be life-long. Hence the enormous importance Plato attaches to early education and most of all to the kind of education we get unconsciously, while our whole being is still plastic, from play-

ing the right kind of games, hearing the right
kind of stories, learning to delight in the right
kind of poetry and music. By such ways as
these a sound social tradition is unconsciously
imbibed; our whole environment is made
pregnant with suggestions of good, and loyalty
to high standards of conduct is made the very
foundation of our character. This conception
of moulding character by working on taste and
imagination is the great theme of the best-
known section of the *Republic*. The same
thoughts dictate the famous doctrine that the
real object of the penal exercise of force is
neither retaliation nor prevention of social
harm nor deterrence from repetition of of-
fences, but " reformation "; even the penalty
of death is an education; its object is to make
the offender a wiser and better man, in the
world to come if not in this.

Of course this whole conception rests on one
great pre-supposition. If all the organized
institutions and habits of the society around
us are to suggest nothing but what is morally
noble, the foundations of society themselves
must have been rightly laid. Our institutions
must themselves be the expression of a true

[65]

estimate of the various goods and they must be preserved from degeneration by the same judgment which has created them. This is why Plato's profoundest conviction in Politics is that human happiness requires that " philosophers," the men who really know what good and evil are, should be " kings," in other words, that the highest wisdom and the supreme social authority should be conjoined. Any departure from this rule means that the direction of social life is in the hands of men who have more or less gravely falsified ideals of what life should be and can be. The institutions and traditions of society thus become debased, a wrong public opinion is created, and characters are inevitably moulded on wrong lines. The further the falsification of the national ideal of character goes, the greater the difficulty in producing the man or woman with the kind of character which makes happiness possible. This explains Plato's rooted objection to " democracy," in the Greek sense of the word, " government by town's meeting." [40] Where there is no authority to control the changing moods of the " crowd," there is really no fixed tradition of living, no recognized " social ideal " of what life should be, but a mere anarchical struggle between inconsistent and competing " ideals," all defective.

Like the rule of " philosophers," the " emancipation of women " is a simple consequence of the general theory. But the very use of the word " emancipation " puts the matter in a false light. Plato's reason for proposing to disregard the distinction of sex in education and in filling public offices is not in the least to " emancipate " the female sex from restrictions. The thought which inspired him and Socrates, — it shocked the more conservative Aristotle — is simply that " the virtue of a woman is the same as that of a man;" [41] moral nobility exhibits itself in both sexes in the same forms, right judgment of good and evil, high honour, self-control and the like. Hence the same educative discipline is applicable to and necessary for both sexes, and, where it succeeds, will in both produce the type of character which ought to be entrusted with authority.

It is a much more important consequence of the theory that there can be no difference in spirit between the laws of public and of private morality. If the real function of the State and its institutions is to create a tradition of noble life into which successive generations of men and women grow as their rightful heritage, the State itself in its dealings with other States, and the diverse classes or orders within the State, in their dealings with one another, must conform to the very same ideal which we wish each budding citizen to take as the standard of his own personal conduct. Whoever holds that what would be "morally" reprehensible for the individual person may be "politically" admirable when done by the official representatives of the State, has broken with the whole view of the reasons for civic loyalty and political subjection characteristic of both Plato and Aristotle. Both are at one on the points that the true greatness of a State is to be measured neither by its material wealth nor by its territory nor by its success in dominating its neighbours, but solely by the personal worth of its citizens, and that the "law of the land" derives its right to respect from its conformity with the moral law; it is not from Greek philosophy, but from the practice of Roman politicians of the evil age after the second Punic war that modern times have borrowed the doctrines of "empire" as an end in itself and of "reasons of state " as superseding regard for right and wrong.[42]

We must not here dwell in detail on the readily accessible sketch of a society organized for the express purpose of producing nobility of character given in the *Republic*. It is more to our purpose to observe that certain parts of the *Republic* and *Laws* are the first examples of a " philosophy of history " in European literature. In many ways the most impressive section of the *Republic* is that (Bk. VIII and the opening pages of Bk. IX), which presents us with a series of sketches of the various defective social constitutions and the types of character they favour, in the order of increasing divergence from the true ideal. We miss the point of the picture if we try to find in it nothing more than an expression of personal bias in favour of " aristocracy " and against " democracy." The real theme is the sinfulness of man, and the whole section might well have for its motto, " sin, when it hath conceived, bringeth forth death." The main thought is that declension in the standard of personal conduct leads inevitably to the lowering and coarsening of the tone of public life and the passing of power into unfit hands.

This, in turn, leads to a still further decline in personal character and so once more to a worse type of national life.

If a society passes through all the possible stages of degeneration until it finally sinks into sheer enslavement to a criminal usurper, the reason is that "education" has been increasingly neglected and the personal moral quality of the typical citizen has consequently suffered. When a State, for example, begins to disregard science and thinking and to overvalue the military qualities of the stout and loyal soldier and sportsman as constituents of manhood, as the Spartans did, it still remains, as things go, a society with a great deal of good in it. The citizens of such a State are much better men than those of one which is given up to the pursuit of wealth or excitement, but it has taken the first fatal step on the downward ladder and is doomed, unless its whole public and private life undergoes a salutary reform, to take the rest. Plato has been, strangely enough, accused of "idealizing" Sparta; it would be nearer the mark to say that behind Agesilaus he saw the shadows of the third-century ephors and of the "tyrant" Nabis. So his alleged bitterness against "democracy" might fairly be called a presentiment of the days when the Athenian rabble were to deify Demetrius Poliorcetes.[43]

No less striking, as a contribution to the philosophical interpretation of history, is the third book of the *Laws*. The growth of a society is here illustrated by the supposition that, at some date long before the dawn of recorded history, the whole population of a district has been wiped out by a flood, except for a few scattered families of shepherds and goatherds in the inaccessible uplands. We have a brilliant picture of the ensuing " dark ages," the very slow recovery of the industrial arts and of writing, the gradual descent of the mountaineers into the fruitful plains as the memory of the ancient flood fades, their aggregation into bodies of growing size, the transition through a nomadic to a settled agricultural way of life and the final formation of monarchies and building of great cities. (This is obviously the source of Aristotle's well known theory of the three stages of social organization, the family, the " village," the " city," only that (1) the details and the intermediate stages are more fully worked out by Plato, (2) that he is alive, as Aristotle is not, to the part played by

the violence of Nature and of man in the development, and (3) that he has a keen sense of
the vast stretches of human life lying behind
all our recorded history which is wanting both
in Aristotle and in the Christian Middle Ages.)

The growth of society has now been traced
down to the age of the wealthy and chivalrous
monarchies of the Homeric poems, and Plato
goes on to illustrate from the traditional stories
of the war against Troy, the subsequent disas-
ters in the confederate States which had prosecuted the war, and the Dorian invasion of the
Peloponnese, the effects of a " world-war " in
the disintegration of old communities and the
rise of new and the radical modification of social institutions. The traditional history of the
three Dorian kingdoms in the Peloponnese is
then made to furnish important lessons in the
evils attendant on mutual jealousies between
neighbour-states and the cultivation of the
spirit of narrow self-aggrandizement. Finally,
to enforce the thesis that neither unqualified
" personal rule " nor unqualified " democracy "
is a desirable state of things, we have a striking sketch of the stories of Persia and Athens
from the time of Cyrus. Both had begun as
communities in which " popular control " had

been blended with something of "personal authority," but in Persia, the "people" have become the mere slaves of a capricious autocrat and in Athens there has been a loss of the sense for "awful rule and right authority," so that the real strength of both has vanished, — a judgment absolutely justified by the events of the half-century after Plato's death.[44]   In both cases the root of the evil is found in "neglect of education." Since the day of the great Darius, every Persian king has been "born in the purple," and has grown up a mere spoiled child; the Athenians began their downward course by assuming that any one man's opinion is as good as any other's in matters of musical and literary taste, and it was not long before they extended the principle to the whole range of national life.

The debt of Christian moralists to Plato is often under-estimated as a result of certain misunderstandings of his doctrine. He, with the Greek moralists in general, is sometimes charged with subordinating the individual unduly to the State, and the "absolute worth of individual souls" is spoken of as a new discovery made by Christianity. Closely connected with this is the popular notion that Plato

is a " socialist " or " communist," a view which
leads to laudation or vituperation according to
the economic leanings of the particular critic.
This may be dismissed as a mere unintelligent
blunder. The whole point of Plato's doctrine
is precisely that the purpose of all the institutions of the State is the production of noble
personal character. It is true that his vocabu-
lary has no technical word for " personality,"
but the absence of the word should not blind
us to the omnipresence of the idea.[45] In
economic matters Plato is no more " socialist "
or " communist " than Aristotle. Even in the
Republic, as attentive reading shows, all the
machinery of the production of wealth is left
in the hands of individuals. What Socrates is
made to insist on is not the " collectivizing "
of capital, but something very different, the
absolute divorce of political power and capital.
There are just two classes, the philosophic
statesmen and their trained executive force, to
whom all property is absolutely proscribed.
They do all the responsible public work and
wield the whole civil and military power of the
State, but they are expected to live in absolute
poverty, receiving nothing but their bare maintenance, and that on a scale appropriate to

men who are all the time on garrison duty.[46] Their life, in fact, is like that of military monks, with the exception that they are expected to " beget children for the State," and we must remember that their unions for this purpose are only formed when the State directs and their partners chosen for them by the official " eugenists." Their life is made harder than it would be under the monastic vow of chastity by this combination of the duty to procreate with the prohibition of all indulgence of parental or conjugal affection.[47] Even in the *Laws,* where the ideal is relaxed by the recognition of family life, Plato is so far from being a " collectivist " that the foundation of his economic system is that every family possesses its own " holding " which it is legally forbidden to alienate or enlarge, and there is an express prohibition of even common cultivation.[48]

A rather less superficial, but still a superficial, criticism is the common one that Plato and the Greek moralists in general have no place in their moral scheme for the specifically " Christian " virtues of self-denial and humility. It would be easy to show that even as regards Aristotle, the accusation is not really fair; as against Plato it is simply false. Here again we are in danger of being misled by mere accidents of linguistic history. Plato has, indeed, not the specific names " self-denial " and " humility," but this does not mean that he does not demand the qualities. In the *Republic*, for example, self-denial of a high order is covered by the name " temperance." Temperance, whether in the individual or in the State, we are told is a " concord " between all " parts " of the soul or all classes in the State, on the question who is to rule and who is to obey. The man who is fitted for the commercial or industrial life must be content with his position and not attempt to thrust himself into the work of a soldier or statesman; the men who have the gifts for the latter occupations must not seek to shirk them and make their private fortunes in business or give themselves up to scholarly leisure. Here we clearly have a demand for very real self-denial. For the ambitious and successful business man it is a true exercise of self-denial to go through life without aspiring to the distinction of being one of the " rulers." The " rulers " . themselves have to make a harder sacrifice. They are expected to forego everything that makes life worth having to the ordinary man. They alone possess not a stiver of property; they live hard in perpetual garrison; they are absolutely cut off from the endearments of family life. All the hardest and most responsible work is laid on them and the only return they get is the consciousness that the work has been well and honourably done. They are the thinkers and men of science of the community, but all through their physical and mental prime they are to be taken from their studies and researches and made to occupy themselves with the dull and exhausting work of administration. It is hard to see how the demand for complete self-abnegation could be made more exacting.

Similarly, the apparent absence of " humility " from the list of virtues is due to the accident that the word which in the Hellenistic Greek of the New Testament means " humble " had in classical Attic the sense of " cringing," and mean cringing is no more a Christian than it was a Greek virtue. But a proper modesty and submissiveness of demeanour towards one's elders and betters was a highly valued quality and finds its place in the *Republic* under the caption of " temper-

[77]

ance." If what is meant by the critics is humility of spirit towards God, rather than proper modesty towards men, Plato not only demands the thing but does not shrink from the suggestions of the word. Perhaps the sentence most often quoted from him throughout later antiquity is the great text of the *Laws:* " God, as the old saw has it, holding in his hand the beginning and end and middles of all things, moves straight round the whole circuit, and with him goes Right the justicer of things that come short of God's law; he who would be happy cleaves to her and follows in her train, in all humility and discipline; but he who, puffed up with conceit or lifted up by wealth and rank or, it may be, by beauty and youthful folly, is all afire with lusts, like one who needs no ruler or guide but is rather sufficient to be a guide to others, is left behind, abandoned of God; in which abandonment he takes to him others like himself, waxes wanton in riot, and is thought by many to be some great one; yet after a little while he makes no scanted amend to Right by the clean ruin of himself, his household and his city." [49] The thought which, more than any other, dominates the *Laws* is just that we are all God's " playthings," and there is really no very great distinction between the puppets who figure as kings and as beggars in the show; what matters is that each should fill his part in the game well.

There is more substance in the criticism often made by Thomists that the real difference between the Platonic and the Christian rule of life is just the difference between " nature " and supernatural " grace." The Platonic ethics exhibit the ideal of all to which unassisted human effort can rise; what Christianity adds *de suo* is just the further transformation of " nature " into " supernature," which is only possible in virtue of the special prevenient and coöperating grace bestowed through Christ and his Church on those who have been " born again of water and the spirit." We shall see directly that this would not be true if it were understood to mean that Plato's outlook is confined to " temporal " or " worldly," as opposed to " eternal " good. It may be doubted whether the criticism can be maintained at all except on the condition of making an impossibly rigid and sharp distinction between grace and nature and holding that all grace is mediated exclusively through the organization of the Church. The first position is hard

to conciliate with the insistence of Thomists
themselves on the point that grace does not
abolish nature but transforms it by lifting it
to a higher level. The second is incompatible
with the tradition which goes back to Augustine, and ultimately to St. Paul, according to
which God never " left himself without a wit-
ness " in the Gentile world, and with the more
generous view of the Alexandrians that God
revealed Himself to the Greeks through Philosophy as He did to the Hebrews through
their prophets. Perhaps the truest thing that
can be said on the point is that what Christianity has contributed entirely of itself is just
the personality of Jesus Christ, the one
source of noble life which is to be found
neither in philosophy nor in prophecy. There
is no virtue, not even those of faith, hope and
charity, which we may not find in germ both
in Greek philosophy and in the Old Testament
Scriptures, but all are transfigured in Christianity by the connection with the Person of
Christ. To take a single example, the " theological " virtue of hope, if it means the attitude
of hopeful aspiration towards a good which
no temporal life can exhaust, is familiar
enough in Plato; it is the note on which the

Phaedo, the *Gorgias,* the *Republic* all end. But this is not exactly the same thing as the more specific Christian hope of eternal life with and through Jesus Christ, any more than the recognition of all men as one family or as creatures of the same Maker is the same thing as the Christian love of a fellow-man as an actual or potential member of the one " body of Christ." [50]

It is not uncommon to hear the Ethic of the Greek moralists, that of Plato in particular, censured as unduly " intellectualistic," and the point of difference from Christianity has actually been sought in the theory that Plato desires to save men from ignorance where Christians desire to save them from sin. The criticism is, in any case, hard to understand, and could moreover be raised by no Christian who had not repudiated the main current of Christian tradition. The alleged intellectualism seems to lie chiefly in the doctrine that ignorance or error is the source of sin, and the formula consequently adopted by both Socrates and Plato that " no one is voluntarily bad." The current criticisms arise from a misunderstanding of these propositions. What is really meant is simply that

he who chooses evil in preference to good
does so not *because of,* but *in spite of* its bad-
ness. He must be deluded, or delude himself,
into the belief that the evil he chooses is a
good before he makes the choice. No one
in his senses would defend a choice by the
argument that the thing chosen was so very
evil, though we think it a sufficient defence
of a choice to urge that the thing chosen is
very good. If this is intellectualism, it is an
intellectualism which is common to Plato with
Aristotle, Augustine, Thomas and Kant. Aristotle's formula that "everyone chooses what
he thinks good, but only the good man always
thinks good what really is good" is a simple
reassertion of the Platonic doctrine, and the
formula of the Christian schoolmen, *quidquid
petitur petitur sub specie boni,* merely repeats
Aristotle. Indeed it is hard to understand
how any man can convince himself that it is
possible to choose evil, not in spite of the fact
that it is evil but precisely because one be-
lieves it to be so.

The saying that "all wrong-doing is involuntary" again is commonly misunderstood. The
meaning is not that our misdeeds are due to
"circumstances beyond our control," and we

are accordingly not to blame for them, but simply that wrong-doing does not lead to that which we all wish to have. We wish for real happiness but sin leads regularly to misery; hence the sinner always gets just what he never wished to have. As Proclus puts it, Plato says that wrong-doing is involuntary, Aristotle that it is voluntary, but there is no real contradiction between the two. For by the " voluntary " Plato means " that for which we really wish," Aristotle means " that which it is in our power to do or leave undone "; hence what is involuntary in Plato's sense may be voluntary in Aristotle's. Through Aristotle the doctrine passes to the Christian Aristotelians of the thirteenth century, so that we find Thomas, for instance, expressly declaring that " every sin arises from a kind of ignorance . . . so that man's will is only secure from sinning when his understanding is secured from ignorance and error." [51] Even the fall of Satan is no exception to the universal rule that every creature in all its acts inevitably aims at its own " natural good." The pride by which the angels fell consisted not in departure from this universal law but in seeking their own good elsewhere than in conformity to the divinely established order of things.[52]

It is hardly necessary to indicate the way in which Plato's ethical doctrines passed into the tradition of the Church. The writings of the earliest Greek Fathers[53] and Apologists naturally draw directly upon him and, to the third century, the works of Philo further provided a model for the reading of Platonism into the Old Testament Scriptures. In the Western Church the Platonic influence was mediated partly by divines like Ambrose whose inspiration comes through Alexandria and the Cappodocians, (Basil and the Gregories), and mainly through the standing tradition derived from Augustine and Boethius. Further there was always the potent influence of the moral and political works of Cicero, themselves mainly academic in spirit, in spite of the use made in some of them of the platonized Stoicism of Panaetius and Posidonius. In the thirteenth century the Neo-Aristotelianism of Thomas made Aristotle's *Ethics* what it has remained ever since, the chief direct source of the official moral philosophy of the Roman Church. In principle this means little more than that the Platonic doctrines continue to

be presented in an arid and formal way and
with a certain admixture of " naturalism." [54]
The revival of Greek learning in the fifteenth
century and the age of " Ciceronianism " which
ensued sent men back again to the fountain-
heads, but the inspiration of the most prominent philosophers of the movement is not
ethical. Giordano Bruno, the most consider-
able figure among them, is an enthusiast, with
more zeal than real knowledge, for the new
vistas in cosmology opened up by the return
to Plato, but the ethics of the *Spaccio della
Bestia* and *Eroici Furori* are naturalistic
rather than Platonic. The " life of measure "
extolled in the *Philebus* and *Laws* would have
been as little to Bruno's taste as the *vita sub
disciplina* from which he apostatized. And if
the Roman Holy Office burned him, the
" Inquisition " established in the *Laws* would
also probably have passed the capital sentence
on him.[55]

In England, where the tradition of Augustine and Boethius was never really broken,
Plato has always been the prime influence in
shaping the moral theory of the national divines. If his influence undergoes a brief
eclipse under the Puritans (whom he resem-

[85]

bles at any rate in moral seriousness), owing
to the prevalence of the Calvinist views about
"total depravity," the eclipse is only brief.
It is from him that Cudworth, Henry More,
John Smith, directly draw the inspiration for
their doctrine of reason, "the candle of the
Lord" in the human mind, as the source of an
eternal and immutable morality, and their
general conception of its contents; and thus
Platonism furnishes the basis at once for their
protest against the ethical naturalism of
Hobbes and for their rejection of the Calvinis-
tic view of the desperate condition of "human
nature after the Fall." Moral philosophy
has, in our own literature, been so closely
connected with divinity that this influence
passes naturally into the ethical classics of the
language, themselves mostly, until quite recently, the works of divines. We trace it in
Samuel Clarke, and, with special emphasis on
the aesthetic side of the doctrine, in Shaftesbury, Hutcheson and their numerous followers;
through Clarke it came direct to Butler, the
greatest philosopher of Anglicanism, who is
ultimately indebted to Plato not only for his
insistence on the absolute authority of the
moral law but for his characteristic account of

the hierarchy of " principles of action," a reproduction, with interesting differences, of the " parts in the soul." [56]   Plato, Clarke and Cudworth are equally the inspiration of the finest of all expositions of rational Ethics in our language, Richard Price's *Review of the Principal Questions in Morals,* which bears on its titlepage a characteristic motto from the *Phaedo.* In the nineteenth century the Platonic influence was obscured, first by the temporary success of Utilitarianism and then by the Aristotelianism of the Oxford group among whom T. H. Green is the central figure, but it seems to be regaining its old importance as Aristotelianism itself, on closer study, is steadily found to be only a rather half-hearted Platonism.

The influence of Plato in Politics has been of two kinds. It has been most permanently transmitted by the channel of Aristotle's *Politics* which, with all their conservatism, dread of social experiment and limitation of outlook, at least conveyed to the thirteenth century the Platonic conceptions of the educational functions of the State and the true ground of political obedience. This explains the fact that the greatest scholastics teach a doctrine of the

basis and limits of sovereignty and its dependence on the "good of the people" which is,
in substance, one with modern "constitutionalism." [57] The constitutional doctrine expounded in Locke's essays on *Civil Government* and transmitted, through Locke, to
Rousseau and the founders of the United
States, is linked up through Hooker, Thomas
and Aristotle's *Politics* with Plato's *Laws,* the
greatest ancient contribution to the theory of
statesmanship. Even the rival "absolutist"
conception of Hobbes and his nineteenth-cen-
tury imitators, the Benthamites, though based
on an anti-social conception of human nature
intended as a direct contradiction of Plato and
Aristotle, in its own way goes back to Plato
too. It enshrines at least one thoroughly Platonic principle, the thought that the State is
made for man, not man for the State. Even
the singularly un-Platonic view of civil society
as a co-partnership for strictly limited ends
begins, in Hobbes, as an attempt to bring political institutions under the principles of the
Roman law of corporations; and we are gradually learning that the whole body of Roman
law was deeply influenced by the law of the
Hellenistic communities, itself shaped very

largely under the influences of the Academic jurisprudence represented for us by Plato's *Laws*.[58] It need hardly be added that all this modern political theorizing has been deeply coloured by developments wholly foreign to the age of Plato. Our constitutionalism has been largely created by the mediaeval attempts to delimit the spheres of civil and spiritual authority, and within the latter to determine the relative position of the Pope and the General Councils. Since in the Platonic " city " civil and spiritual authority are conjoined, in it many of the problems for which our various theories, from ultra-montanism to " philosophic anarchy," are meant as solutions, do not arise and do not exist.

On the other hand, the famous " paradoxes " of the *Republic*, the rule of " philosophers," the abolition, so far as the rulers are concerned, of family life and property, and the removal of the sex-disqualification, have had little influence on the general course of grave political and constitutional thinking, but have constantly supplied inspiration to original minds dissatisfied with the social conditions of their own day. Plato's *Republic* may fairly be called the " onlie begetter " of the host of literary Utopias from Sir Thomas More and Campanella down to the fantastic romances of writers like H. G. Wells. But the " paradoxes " are not the really important thing in Plato's political thought. What he really cares about is chiefly the abolition of the political influence of mere wealth and rank, the connection of political power with proved character and wisdom, the elimination of jobbery from public life, and the imposing of public duties on those who are fittest to bear them, independently of sex. In the *Republic* there is a strong element of humour which leads Socrates, the main speaker, of set purpose, to make his points in the most paradoxical way. It may be gravely doubted whether Plato ever imagined that he would be supposed by the dull-witted to be prophesying the detailed arrangements of a New Jerusalem, and more than doubted whether he would have approved of the introduction of the New Jerusalem, by sudden revolution, to a society wholly unprepared for it. Men who do their best with the means available to them to put power into the hands of character and intelligence, to diminish the opportunities for jobbery, to give the young of both sexes a rational education and to teach them that marriage and the procreation of children are grave responsibilities are more true to the spirit of Platonism than lighthearted devisers of schemes of "social regeneration." There is more true Platonism in the remark that "we must *educate* our masters" than in a thousand such patent schemes for the perfecting of human nature. Least of all have the emancipators who propose to make short work of all institutions which limit the individual's freedom to do just as he likes, any right to inscribe the name of Plato on their banners. Ruskin, when he said that in his Community of St. George there would be "no liberty at all," meant something which is thoroughly Platonic; Shelley's crusade against all that calls itself law and authority, for all Shelley's love of the imaginative poet in Plato, is a mere glorification of what Plato thought most deadly in "democracy." Indeed, we might perhaps say that the best of all commentaries on the *Laws* and *Republic* is *Fors Clavigera,* — read, of course, with discrimination. What Plato really cares for is that a man should be helped and not hindered by social regulations in finding the "vocation" in which he can best promote the common good, and that

having found it, he should make it the one
business of his life to fructify in that vocation
to the utmost of his power, — an ideal, familiar enough to Christians, but utterly opposed both to the mechanical " regimentation "
dear to Socialists and ultra-Tories, and to the
" go-as-you-please " ideal of the Anarchist, or
his half-hearted brother the " philosophical
Radical."

The glad acceptance of one's " vocation " is
not only the true service of man, it is also the
service of God. At this point Plato's morality
makes that contact with religion without which
any morality withers into a dreary formalism.
Of Plato's theology something will be said in
the next chapter; here we are concerned not
with his speculative doctrine of God but with
the practical faith by which he would have a
good man's whole life governed. This practical faith is a very simple but a very real
thing, and it should be noted that it is just
what we still mean by " faith." The whole
doctrine of the scheme of goods on which Platonic morality is based requires the direction
of life in absolute obedience to convictions
which the good man may be quite unable to
prove, but he must none the less be absolutely

loyal to them. The absolute subordination of all other good to the " good of the soul " is founded on the convictions that the human soul has an eternal destiny, and that the order of the universe has been so disposed by a perfectly wise and righteous God that our future happiness or misery is precisely adjusted to our present character and conduct. Few things in Plato are better known to the average general reader than the splendid imaginative pictures of future life and judgment to come which conclude the *Phaedo,* the *Gorgias* and the *Republic.* But it would be hard to say how far the Orphic-Pythagorean mythology of reincarnation which Plato adopts as the setting for these stories is meant to be taken as more than fanciful. Possibly he could not have answered the question himself, but he has taken care to warn us against literalism by the caution that the details of his myths are no more than " likely stories," and it is notable that when he comes to the construction of a theology in the *Laws,* the great doctrines of Providence, immortality and judgment to come are set forth without the trappings of mythology. What he is in dead earnest in maintaining is that the universe is under the gov-

ernment of a Providence which ignores
nothing and forgets nothing and that a man's
fate all through eternity depends on his
character.

Historically, perhaps, the Platonic eschatology is important chiefly as the source of
Christian doctrines about Purgatory. For
heaven, the Christian imagination could draw
on the pictures of the Apocalypse of John the
Divine; the same source furnished, though
more scantily, suggestions of the fate of the
finally impenitent. We need not suppose that
the apocalyptic " lake of fire and brimstone "
had to be eked out by reminiscences of the
tormentors " of fiery and savage aspect " in
the myth of Er. But the Scriptures do little
to furnish any picture of a place of purgation
for the faulty but not wholly " lost." The
humanist Friar in *The Cloister and the Hearth*
seems right in saying that " all we know about
Purgatory " comes to us through Gregory the
Great from the sixth book of Virgil's *Aeneid,*
and that Virgil, in his turn, has taken his information direct from the Platonic eschatological myths.

In another way, Plato's eschatology is still
a powerful force in our own divinity. There

are few hints in Plato of anything like an unending hell. He now and then speaks as though he contemplated the possibility that a sinner may prove quite irreclaimable, and, in the Platonic doctrine, the soul that is " incurable " is necessarily in a perpetual hell. But he thinks of the incurables as a very few, and those for the most part famous " tyrants," great bad men who have been able to set themselves above the law and gratify on the grand scale the " wild beast " which lurks in us all. With the majority of sinners it is otherwise, and for them the Platonic " hell " is a place of temporary detention where they learn obedience by the things they suffer. The tendency of the Platonizing Christians, Origen, Gregory of Nyssa, Scotus Erigena, to mention only names from antiquity, has always been towards some form of the doctrine of " universalistic " restoration. We may note the same thing among more modern Christian divines of our own speech. Devotion to Plato regularly goes hand in hand with revolt against the more merciless forms of the doctrine of " damnation." It is true that here Augustine, in the main the great source of Platonism in Western Christianity, is on the other side. The terrible doctrine of the *massa perditionis* is a strange inheritance from the man to whom we also owe the maintenance of the Platonic tradition. But it was true of Augustine more fully than of most men that two spirits did " suggest him still " and most of us would probably admit that his conceptions about the *massa perditionis* did not come from his " better angel."

IV. PLATO THE THEOLOGIAN

IN preaching a practical religion of faith in God's righteous governance and in the eternal destiny of the soul Plato was treading in the footsteps of Socrates and Pythagoras. Theology, as a body of doctrine about God claiming to be capable of proof, was his own creation and first appears in the tenth book of the *Laws*, the great work of Plato's old age. Here we meet for the first time in history with the outlines of what has come to be known as " natural " theology. To the Christian the adjective suggests a contrast with " revealed " or " historical " theology, which rests on the authority of a real or supposed direct communication from God made at a definite place and time to a definite historical person. But the original meaning of the name " physical " or " natural " theology was different. We owe the phrase to Cicero's contemporary, the famous antiquarian Marcus Terentius Varro, who distinguished three kinds of theology, or " discourse about God," poetical, civil, and natural or philosophical. Poetical theology means what we call the "classical mythology," the body of tales of the gods and their doings to be found in the Greek poets and their Roman imitators. Civil theology is concerned with the official worship of the State and consists in a proper knowledge of the festivals and fasts of the calendar, the ceremonies required for each of them and the persons by whom these rites must be performed. Philosophical or natural theology is the doctrine of God taught by philosophers as an integral part of the truth about the reality of things. It is only this last kind of theology which Varro regards as having any claim to be true. The established view about mythology, as early as the days of Herodotus, was that it had been made up by the poets, whose sole object in their stories was not to instruct but to interest and amuse. Civil theology, again, has nothing to do with truth or falsehood; it is the creation of the magistrate who sanctions certain feasts and other ceremonies with a view to nothing beyond their social utility. As Scaevola the Pontiff had said, in a very Roman spirit, there is only one kind of theology (the civil) which is of any social utility, and it is not true.[59]

Natural theology, then, meant originally a doctrine about God which is neither imaginative fiction nor socially useful fiction but science, and such a doctrine was attempted for the first time by Plato in the *Laws*. His motive in constructing it is primarily a moral one. He holds that there are certain beliefs which are ruinous to character, and that they may be reduced in the end to three. The soul-destroying heresies are (1) the belief that there is no God at all, (2) the belief that though there may be a God or gods, at least there is no moral government of the world, " the gods do not concern themselves with mens' affairs," (3) the belief that there may be such a divine government, but that the impenitent sinner can escape judgment by buying the divine favour with costly offerings. It is of the first importance to the legislator, who aims at producing noble character, that such beliefs should, if possible, be shown to be false, and Plato thinks he can supply the necessary proof. Of the three, the first, simple atheism, is the least deadly; the second is worse, since it charges the gods with ignorance or levity or both; the third is worst of all, for it imputes downright moral corruption to them. It would be better to believe in no kind of God at all than to believe in a careless God, and it is better to believe in a careless God than to believe in a venal one. An honest atheist is a far better man than a " believer " who builds churches or finances missions out of the profits of a successful " corner " or a gambling " flotation."

Against the atheist Plato has an argument which he thinks conclusive and sufficient to establish at once the existence of God and the immortality of the soul. The main principle on which it turns had been briefly introduced in the *Phaedrus*,[60] but the elaboration of the argument in detail and its employment as a reply to the atheist are peculiar to the *Laws*. We may condense the reasoning as follows. There is no more palpable fact than the universality of motion; there has always been motion in the world and there always will be. But all motion is of one of two kinds: it is either communicated from without or originated from within. And communicated motions must in the end always be started by something which is moved from within. No series of movements can be *started* except by something which moves " spontaneously." The " motion which moves itself " must be logically and causally prior to the " motion which can move other things but cannot move itself." Thus the very existence of nature presupposes the existence of one or more such fountains of movement. Also, what " moves itself " must be imperishable because it does not depend for its activity on any external source but contains the conditions of its own persistence wholly within itself. Now language has already provided us with a name for the " motion which can move itself; " we call it " soul." (I.e. it is by ability or inability to initiate movement from within that we discriminate the " animate " from the inanimate. Hence in Plato's psychology the formal definition of a " soul " is that it is a " movement which can move itself.")

The motions of soul are causally prior to all bodily motions, and the motions of soul are such things as thoughts, memories, wishes, hopes, fears. Our argument thus shows that all the " motions " of which physical science takes account, translation, rotation, contrac-

tion, expansion and the rest, are causally dependent on "motions of the soul," and the
great oversight of the early men of science lay
in taking the physical motions as ultimate and
self-explanatory. Ionian science, without in-
tending it, prepared the way for the atheism
which holds that there is no purpose or intelligence behind the scheme of physical nature.[61]
Now souls are either good or bad, and a good
soul, in proportion as it is good, will initiate
orderly and regular movements, a bad soul
shows its own internal want of order in the
disorderliness of the movements it initiates.
But the great and far-reaching movements in
nature, those of the heavenly bodies, are strictly
regular and orderly; disorderly movements,
"convulsions of nature," are the exceptions and
their range is limited. We infer then that the
dominant souls to which the cosmical movements are due are good and orderly, and the
supreme soul of all (no doubt this means the
one which is responsible for the most universal and regular movement of all, that of the
"heaven of the fixed stars") is a perfectly
good soul. Since there are disorderly movements in nature, this cannot be the only soul;
there must be many souls, or at the least more

than one, to account for the disturbance of order, but the disorderly souls are inferior and subordinate.[62]   This is Plato's proof of the existence of God, and we must note two things about it.

(1) The argument, as it stands, is not necessarily an argument for the existence of only one God. If there is a plurality of perfectly orderly motions, there will be a corresponding plurality of perfectly good souls.   Hence Plato speaks all through the reply to the atheist of "gods" rather than of God.   At most the argument would go to prove that there is one soul which is the greatest and best of all, a supreme "God of gods."   That Plato was personally a monotheist, however, seems plain from the fact that when he is speaking with most moral fervour and earnestness, he so regularly says not "gods" but God, just as Socrates in the *Apology* always speaks of his mission to the souls of his fellow-Athenians as laid on him not by Apollo, nor by "the gods," but by God.[63] (2) Also we note that God is definitely said to be "the best *soul.*"   It is important to remember that, according to Plato, God is a soul and not a Form and that a soul is a "motion

[103]

which moves itself." This is really the last word of Platonism on the question how things come to " partake of " Forms; they do so because God apprehends the Forms, and his apprehension of them inspires his " orderly " motions.

The confutation of the atheist leads readily to the silencing of the other two classes of heretics. If the " best soul " exists, to say that he does not concern himself with mundane affairs is as much as to assert that he is either ignorant of them or neglectful of them. But in a perfectly good soul there is no room for ignorance or carelessness or wilful neglect. In particular it is singularly foolish to hold that God provides for the orderliness and regularity of the great cosmic motions but thinks the behaviour of man too trival a matter for his attention. It is just in taking account of so-called minor things and small matters that high intelligence and character show themselves. The " best soul," we may be sure, neglects nothing at all as beneath its notice. It is only inferior souls, even among men, which " cannot be bothered " with the supposedly little matters. And the suggestion that the vigilance of the

best soul can be bribed to connive at our misdeeds is no more than blasphemy against its
goodness. Some people talk as though the
work of attending to all these affairs must be
infinitely troublesome to God. But the truth
is rather that God has arranged for them by
the establishment of a single law of remark-
able simplicity, a law of what we might call
"gravitation." In the spiritual, as in the
physical world, it is the universal law that
"like is attracted to like." A man, as he becomes better or worse, is drawn into the com-
pany of souls of like mind with himself, and
this law operates through all time and all
the succession of lives and deaths. Hence the
man who persists in impiety and wickedness,
finds himself throughout all time in the com-
pany of souls of the same type, and so "does
and has done to him," what befits such society.
Nothing more is needed to ensure the reward-
ing of every man according to his work. It
is notable that we have here the substance of
the eschatological myths of the earlier dialogues without a word of the imaginative
background of "transmigration" or the special
penalties of the hell or purgatory of the *Re-*

public or *Gorgias;* hence we are probably right if we suppose that these pictorial details form no part of Plato's serious belief.[64]

To appreciate the full importance of this section of the *Laws,* we must bear in mind that the refutation of these heresies blocks out the main problems with which " natural " theology has ever since concerned itself, the being and attributes of God, the providential government of the world, the immortality of the soul and the judgment to come. If we take for comparison the great *Summa contra Gentiles* of Thomas, which aims at proving all those doctrines which are demonstrable by unassisted reason and refuting the current objections against those which can only be conveyed to us by a specific revelation, we see that Thomas' first book is given up to the demonstration of the being of God and of the principal divine attributes. The second book deals with the creation in general and its constituent parts, angels, human souls, the relation of the soul to the body, the proofs of the soul's immortality. In the third book we come to the problems of sin, and the moral nature of man, providence and miracle, followed by a general account of the contents of the divine law. So far we are proceeding on strictly Platonic lines in the selection of our problems. The only part of the work which falls outside the limits marked by Plato is the concluding section of the third book on divine grace, and the fourth book which deals with the mysteries of the Trinity and Incarnation, the sacraments instituted as means of grace and the final state of the saved and lost, all matters, according to the Thomist theory of knowledge, definitely outside the range of natural reason.

So again, it would be a fair remark that Plato's three cardinal doctrines of natural theology correspond closely to the three " great postulates " of Kant's ethical theory, " God, immortality and freedom." [65] We may remark, too, that Plato's proof of the existence of God is a combination of two lines of argument which Kant and other modern philosophers have distinguished, the so-called " cosmological " proof, the argument that since something exists there must be a " necessary " being, and the argument from " design." The two lines of reasoning coalesce in Plato's treatment because he finds his necessary being in a supreme " soul " which shows its perfection by the wisdom and goodness of the motions it originates. The whole argument is thus of the type which the schoolmen correctly called *a posteriori*, that is, it is an argument from the existence and character of an effect to those of its cause. (Kant's unscholarly use of the technical terms *a priori* and *a posteriori*, which leads him to regard the cosmological proof and the argument from design as *a priori*, is singularly unfortunate.) There can be only one possible argument for the existence of God which would be *a priori* in the school-men's sense, the argument that consideration of the very meaning of the notion " God " is enough to show that the proposition " God does not exist " is a contradiction in terms. This is the famous " ontological " argument, first stated with great subtlety by St. Anselm in the twelfth century, rejected in the thirteenth by Thomas as fallacious, subsequently revived, but without Anselm's subtlety, by Descartes in his *Fifth Meditation* and accepted as valid though incomplete by Leibniz, but generally discredited for modern philosophers by the slashing onslaught of Kant in the *Critique of Pure Reason*. This " ontological " proof has no counterpart in the " natural theology " of antiquity.[66]

[108]

There is another side, which must not be passed over, to Plato's creation of theology as a science. We owe to him the first proposal to treat " heretical pravity " as a crime and to erect an Inquisition to deal with the offence. To be sure, there were laws at Athens against " impiety," but in the ancient Hellenic world " impiety " did not mean disbelief in a creed, for there were no dogmas or creeds in the religion of an Hellenic State. The official religion was altogether a matter of ceremonial cultus, and " impiety " meant disrespect of the official cultus. This was, of course, an offence to the State which authorized the cultus. It is as certain as anything can be that no expression of opinion about theological matters was an indictable offence in any Greek State. We must not be misled on this point by the facts that certain philosophers were called to account for " impiety " and that Socrates was formally convicted of the offence. In the three most famous instances, those of Anaxagoras, Socrates, Aristotle, the real motive of the proceedings was political. Anaxagoras was attacked as the friend and instructor of Pericles, Socrates was marked out for suspicion by his notorious friendship with Alcibiades, and Aristotle suffered for his personal connection with the Macedonian regent Antipater.[67]

We must not blink the fact that it was actually Plato, who first proposed to make heretical opinions criminal. There is really nothing in this to be surprised at. Plato's reason for providing the city of the *Laws* with an " official " theology is simply his conviction that certain " heresies " are poisonous to character. He would have been false to this conviction if he had not gone on to propose penalties for the circulation of the poison. More distressing than this mere recognition of " heresy " as a crime is the encouragement given to informers and delators by the provision that any good citizen who knows of a case of the breach of the law must report it to the magistrates, and a magistrate who neglects to take action on such a report may himself be prosecuted for " impiety " at the instance of the " common informer." [68] No cognizance is taken of anything but overt speech or action, and the informer against the heretic must have been present in person when the alleged offence was committed. The inquiry is to be undertaken by the highest court of the State, on which eminent men of science have their seats, so that there would be little risk of proceedings like those against Galileo. Plato's inquisitors are not supposed to employ either tortures or cajoleries to extract confessions from accused parties. But the penalties are severe. The minimum sentence for the convicted man is five years' detention in the "House of Correction," where he is not to see any one except members of the Supreme Council of the State, who will do their best to convert him from his error. A second conviction is always to be followed by death.[69]

This is the penalty for offenders whose guilt is not further aggravated by evil living or hypocrisy. The worst kinds of heretic, the hypocrite, the evil-liver, and above all the impostor who preys on the superstitions of other men, are to be confined for life in severe "penal servitude" and their bodies cast out unburied at death; they are, in fact, to be treated as "dead in law" from the moment of conviction, though care must be taken that their innocent families do not suffer for their offence. Modern repugnance to legislation of this kind is probably largely due to doubt about the possibility of real knowledge of things divine. Plato holds that the knowledge

[111]

is possible, and that it is of the highest importance for the formation of character. If we
grant the premisses, it is hard to escape from
Plato's conclusion except by the doubtful plea
that "persecution" always does more to
spread than to repress error.

Plato's principles in these matters are precisely those still followed by the Roman
Catholic Church. The "right to persecute"
is based on the assumption that the persecutor
is possessed of assured truth in matters which
concern man's eternal happiness, and the perse-
cuted in deadly error. Hence neither Plato
nor the Roman Church can really be met by
the argument that they themselves regard
"persecution" as wrong when it is the heretic
who persecutes *them*. It is strictly logical to
condemn the penalizing of truth but to approve
the penalizing of error. Plato would clearly
have had no sympathy with the rival theory
acted on by Tudor sovereigns, that *cuius regio,
eius religio,* that is, that the "sovereign" has
a right to enforce any theology he pleases,
irrespective of its truth, merely because it is
his. But he would have found a point of contact with the doctrine of Innocent III. that
heretics may properly be visited with the

penalties of treason, since they are traitors
to Jesus Christ and this is the greatest of all
possible treasons.[70]

The Platonic theology undergoes significant
modifications in the hands of Aristotle. Aristotle, like his master, is convinced that a " science of God " is possible, and regards this
science as the crown of all philosophical thinking. He also accepts the general principle of
the argument from motion, the visible effect,
to its cause. But he does not accept the
Platonic identification of God with the supreme
" motion which moves itself." Refining further on Plato, he argues that in all cases of
apparent " motion from within " we can distinguish between a constituent which " sets
in motion " and one which " is set in motion."
When an animal is said to move itself this
means that its " soul " sets its body moving;
the " soul " is, in this relation, mover and not
moved, the body moved and not mover. Following up this line of thought, Aristotle is led
to conclude that the explanation of the cosmic
motions requires us to go behind the " self-
moving motion " which Plato had treated as
ultimate. In the things which exhibit unbroken, uniform, spontaneous movement (the

" celestial spheres " of the astronomical theory adopted by Aristotle), there must be a real distinction between the celestial body, the " sphere," which is moved, and the " separate " incorporeal intelligence which " moves it." Every " sphere " will have such a " separated intelligence " as its " unmoved mover." At the head of the whole hierarchy of these " unmoved movers " there will be the " intelligence " which causes the all-embracing " diurnal movement " of the " sphere " of the fixed stars. *This* supreme " unmoved mover " is the God of Aristotle's philosophy, on whom " the whole heaven depends." It will be seen that by making God an " unmoved " mover, Aristotle definitely takes him out of the class of " souls." For a " soul " is not an " unmoved " mover. It moves the body to act, but is also itself " moved " by the objects which it apprehends and desires. So far as this, Aristotle's refinement is accepted by the Neo-Platonists and the mediaeval Christian thinkers, whether Platonist or Aristotelian.[71]

But Aristotle's modification of Platonism does not stop here. The question arises what *kind* of being we must ascribe to the supreme " unmoved mover." Since God is an intelligence, we must ascribe to him a life of thought and intelligence; but since he is a " separate intelligence," " without body, parts or passions," the divine intelligence cannot employ itself in the regulation of non-rational appetition by rational rule. This activity of " practice," the regulation of appetition by intelligence, is precisely what our moral life is. God, having no sensuous appetitions, then, cannot live the life of " practice " at all; he is not a moral being and it is absurd to ascribe to him the " moral " virtues, such as purity or justice.[72] His intelligence must employ itself entirely in " contemplation " or " specula- tion;" it must be an intellectual vision which is itself its own end, or satisfaction, not an out-going activity which " produces " some- thing beyond itself. Further, the eternal self-sameness of God requires that his con- templation should be unbroken by any diver- sion of it from one object to another. God must be rapt in the eternal contemplation of a single object adequate to occupy his per- fect intelligence, and there is no such object other than God himself. The divine life is thus an eternal self-contemplation, a " think- ing of thinking," to which we make a distant approximation not in our moral striving but in the pursuit of scientific truth for its own sake.

It follows that though God is the source of the life and movement of the universe, he is actually unaware of the existence of the world which he " moves." Aristotle tries to illustraté this relation by saying that God moves the world as the object of a man's love moves the lover. We shall do him no injustice if we say that the meaning is that God is to the world much what the Princess of Tripoli was to Jeffrey Rudel, or that the world's desire of God is precisely that " desire of the moth for the star " of which Shelley speaks. This means that Aristotle's theology has no room at all for the Platonic conceptions of God as exercising a providential care for the world or as the righteous judge of men. Still less is there room in such a theory for the great Christian conception that the movement of the soul towards God is really a response to the movement from the other side of the unrelenting and unwearied " love that will not let us go." Aristotle is the philosophical father of arid and naturalistic Deism, as Plato is of ethical Theism.

This lapse into naturalism in theology has

its momentous consequences for Aristotelian ethics. Moral goodness is still conceived in the main on the Platonic lines and Aristotle is emphatic on the indispensability of character for happiness. But, with the divorce between ethics and theology, character, though still a necessary, ceases to be a sufficient condition of happiness, and becomes something secondary.[73] We must be morally good men, because without moral goodness we could have neither the personal freedom from internal distraction nor the orderly and civilized " social environment " necessary for the pursuit of our scientific studies, but it is in these studies and in these alone that Aristotle, unlike Plato, finds the truly divine element in human life. To Plato's mind the man who is trying to mould his own character into conformity to the ideal of moral good, or to embody that ideal in laws and institutions for the good of his fellow citizens, is " following God," imitating in his own degree the providential solicitude of God for the good of all the creatures. With Aristotle the " imitation of God " is confined to a few specially endowed " intellectuals," and the life of moral endeavour loses its highest inspiration. It is not by "bearing the cross," as the rulers in the *Republic* have to bear it, but by studying metaphysics and cosmology and enjoying "classical" music that we come, on Aristotle's theory, to "wear the crown." It is this which gives Aristotle's moral doctrine the "this-world" character which has often been remarked. The letter of the ethical formulae is true to Plato, but the "spirit and the life" have departed from them. In an Aristotelian society men would, of course, practise "justice," but they would do so peremptorily; no one would "hunger and thirst justice," no one would "follow after holiness" with the passion which breathes in the pages of the *Laws* and *Republic*.

All these considerations may serve to show the difficulty of the task before Albert and Thomas when they undertook to substitute Aristotle for Plato, seen through the eyes of Augustine, as the basis of a definitely Christian philosophy. There were, indeed, fundamental points on which divergence from Aristotle was absolutely necessary. A Christian philosophy could not surrender the position that God knows and cares for all his creatures and acts as a righteous judge of men, and that

the service and imitation of God is not confined
to a little aristocracy of superior intellect.
Still less could there be any tampering with
the doctrine of grace or the thought that if
we can love God, it is only because God " first
loved us." All these positions would have
been much more in accord with Plato than
with Aristotle. But there was a stronger motive for the thirteenth-century revolution in
philosophy than even the enthusiasm for the
newly-recovered scientific works of Aristotle.
It lay in certain features of Plato's real or
supposed theory of the soul. Plato had in-
cidentally said in the *Phaedo* that the " saints "
who attain final beatitude live " without
bodies," and this was felt to contradict the
orthodox doctrine of the resurrection. The
Origenist speculations about pre-existence and
re-birth, which had also fallen under ecclesias-
tical condemnation,[74] were based on Platonic
myths. Even if these particular difficulties
could have been got over, the source of the
trouble was deeper. Aristotle alludes to a
psychological view that the union of soul and
body is as loose and accidental as that of
sailor and ship; the schoolmen, who knew no
Platonic dialogue except the *Timaeus,* held

that the reference is to the doctrine of Plato.[76] (In point of fact, no such statement is to be found in Plato, nor does Aristotle hint that his reference is meant for the Academy.) It is clear that a psychology of this kind is quite incompatible with any view of man's ultimate destiny to be found in the New Testament. Aristotle's own theory that the individual soul is the " Form " or " formative principle " of the individual body lends itself more readily to theological orthodoxy, though, to make it compatible with the doctrine of the resurrection, it too requires a reinterpretation which might have surprised Aristotle. Still it seems clear that it is precisely this psychological formula which constitutes Aristotle's superiority over Plato in the eyes of Thomists in general.

The line taken by Thomas was to accept the main outlines of Aristotle's metaphysics and physics, but to avoid all the more naturalistic implications, which had been made prominent by commentators from Alexander of Aphrodisias in the third century to Averroes in the twelfth. In this way the substance of Platonic " natural theology " is retained under the appearance of strict adherence to Aristotelian formulae. Thomism thus emerges as

a substantive philosophy which, in spite of its
enormous debt to Aristotle, is neither the Neo-
Platonized Peripateticism of Averroes nor the
Peripateticism of Alexander nor that of Aristotle himself, but something different from, and
conceivably superior to, them all. The skill
with which the reïnterpreting is done is admirable, but the Aristotle who emerges from it
is, in many ways, the creation of his Christian
interpreter.

One or two examples may be given in illustration. The conception of God as the " unmoved first mover " is retained, and the
Thomist " proofs of God's existence " are all
Aristotelian and open with the Aristotelian
argument for the necessity of a single eternal
" First Mover." [76]   But, as a Christian,
Thomas has to abandon the Aristotelian conception of a deity wrapped up in exclusive
contemplation of himself and unaware of the
existence of anything else. Hence he sets himself to show that though God " primarily and
per se apprehends only himself," yet in appre-
hending his own being he also knows all other
things, since they are all effects of his own
being, and adequate knowledge of a cause
involves knowledge of its effects. The

" nerve " of the argument is the conception of causality as a relation of " mirroring " in which the effect is an imperfect " reflection " or " image " of the cause. This conception is a characteristic philosopheme of the Neo-Platonists and comes to Thomas from Proclus, through Dionysius.[77] It is indispensable for the further vindication of the doctrines of Providence and the moral government of the world. Similarly, though Aristotle's rather one-sided exaltation of science at the expense of " practice " is the foundation of the whole mediaeval doctrine of the superior felicity of the " contemplative " life, Thomas is careful to reunite religion and morality by insistence on the point that the " virtues of action " after all are to be found in God.[78] The thought, which underlies the proof of this position, that the characters of an effect must be found in the corresponding cause, if not exactly as they exist in the effect, still in some " more excellent " way, is again specifically Neo-Platonic and forms part of the theory of causality elaborated by Proclus. (It is to Proclus also that Descartes really owes this view of causation, on which the whole argument of the *Third Meditation* turns, though the principle is declared in the *Meditations* to be obvious by the "natural light.")

So when we come to the doctrine of creation, Thomas is obliged to revert to a position which is far more Platonic than Aristotelian. Neither Plato nor Aristotle had taught what Thomas regards as the true doctrine, guaranteed by revelation, that the whole universe was created "from nothing" a few thousand years ago.[79] Aristotle had expressly taught that the universe is without beginning or end; he had attacked Plato for appearing to think otherwise in the *Timaeus,* though the general tradition of the Academics from the first was that the language of the dialogue about the "creation" of the universe is not to be taken literally. Even with this proviso, however, Plato's doctrine comes much nearer orthodoxy than Aristotle's. For Plato, at any rate, teaches "creation" in the sense that he regards the existence of the whole universe and everything in it as an effect of one single cause, the divine goodness, exactly as Thomas himself does. The universe, in fact, is an imperfect "mirroring" or "image" of the goodness of its maker. Aristotle, on the other hand, makes the universe a resultant of two equally

[123]

eternal causes, God, the source of the motion by which "Form" or "structure" is evoked or induced, and the structureless "first matter," itself not actually any of the things we know, but yet the "potentiality" of them all, from which or upon which the First Mover evokes or superinduces "Form."[80] Thomas retains the Aristotelian "first matter," but, in a very un-Aristotelian spirit, makes it itself a creation of God, though the creation of a mere "potentiality" seems at least hard to conceive.

Here again the thought is really Neo-Platonic. It was the Neo-Platonists who, in their synthesis of Plato and Aristotle, elaborated the doctrine that the higher any cause stands in the scale of being, the lower down the scale do its effects extend. A consequence is that "first matter," the very bottom rung of the ladder, is explained by Proclus to be itself an effect of the transcendent "One" or Deity who is at the top of the scale.[81] Creation, in the philosophical sense of the dependence of everything other than God, for both its existence and its character, on God and solely on God, is thus saved by reading the Neo-Platonist theories about causation into Aristotle.

The further difficulty that, even with this interpretation, Aristotle cannot be made to teach
"creation" in the sense of a beginning of
things at a time distant by a finite interval
from the present, is evaded by the ingenious,
though really quite illegitimate, suggestion
that when Aristotle insists on the "eternity"
of motion he is only arguing *ad homines*. He
is not giving his own opinion but showing that
motion cannot have begun in the fashion
supposed by certain earlier thinkers.[82]   This
interpretation puts Aristotle in the favourable
position of having left undetermined a question which, according to Thomas, can only be
determined by the authority of a revelation
inaccessible to "the philosopher."

The Thomist doctrine of the "rational soul"
is a still more striking example of ingenious
interpretation.   If Plato's eschatology contemplates no "resurrection of the body," there
can be no doubt that it teaches the immortality
of the soul.   It is doubtful whether genuine
Aristotelianism is compatible with either.
The whole trend of Aristotle's *de Anima* is
frankly naturalistic.   The soul is treated
throughout as the "form" of the connected
living body or the "actualization" of its

" capacities." Rationality is the final stage
in this process of " actualization," and Aristotle is emphatic on the point that it only
emerges — in us at any rate — as the last
stage of a development. The natural inference
would be that with the death of the organism
the soul also comes to an end. Yet at the end
of the work, Aristotle tells us in a few broken
sentences, which have been and still remain a
standing puzzle for his interpreters, that there
is an " intelligence " which is not a product
of development but the active cause of the
whole development, and that this alone is
" imperishable." Elsewhere he says of " intelligence " that it is the only thing in us which
comes " from out-of-doors," and the context
shows the meaning to be that it is the one
element in our make-up which is not derived
by generation from our parents. It is doubtful whether any ingenuity of exegesis will
make these sentences fit coherently into his
general psychological scheme, and it must
consequently remain doubtful whether Aristotle means to assert any kind of personal
immortality, though it is going too far to say,
with most modern expositors, that he means
to deny it. It is at least possible that he,

like most men, was not entirely consistent
with himself.

Thomas has then the difficult task of finding
an exegesis which will free Aristotle from all
suspicion of having believed anything incompatible with revealed truth. His task is the
more difficult in that he is compelled to reject
a convenient doctrine of the contemporary
Augustinianism, that of the "plurality of sub-
stantial forms." This doctrine allows us to
believe in the existence of what Aristotle calls
the "form" of the living body and in its
perishability at death, and yet to hold the
immortality of the "reasonable" soul. It
amounts to the view that man's soul is a complex thing and that those parts of the complex
which only serve to control the behaviour of
the body perish with the body's death, — the
doctrine hinted at in Plato's *Republic* and expounded at length in the *Timaeus*.

Thomas, however, is too sound an Aristotelian to accept a theory of this kind. A composite individual "substance" is always a
combination of *this* definite "form" with *this*
definite "matter." To allow that the "form"
itself might be composite would be equivalent
to denying the personal individuality of the

man, and to deny that would be philosophically impossible as well as fatal to Christian faith. The Thomist, therefore, for reasons of philosophy as well as of faith, has to adopt a different line. He needs to argue that though the soul is precisely what Aristotle called it, the " form " of the body, yet, because it is an intelligent and self-conscious " form," it may continue to exist after the severance of its connection with the body, though it will then be in an " incomplete " and unnatural state, and we must look for its final destiny to a reunion with the revivified body of which it is the " form." Thus we safeguard the interests of religion by getting in the immortality of the soul and all its practical consequences, while our strict adhesion to the Aristotelian conception of a soul as *the* " form " of a given body enables us at once to avoid any splitting up of the unity of human personality and also to anticipate the very " resurrection of the flesh " which it is so hard to conciliate with the Platonic conception that the body is only a temporary instrument " used " by the soul which *is* the real man.

Yet it is hard to believe that Aristotle, who wrote that " if the body were all one eye,

seeing would be its soul," would have recognized his own psychology in its Thomist
re-statement, and it is clear that, as regards
the practical religious implications of the doctrine of immortality, Thomas is really in
accord with Plato. If Aristotle ever contemplated the possibility of a felicity to be obtained
" after this present life," at any rate it is clear
from his silence that he took no great interest
in the matter. The felicity he really cares
about, at its very highest, is a felicity to be
enjoyed in this world. Thomas uses the Aristotelian exaltation of the " speculative life "
to prove that the supreme felicity of man can
consist in nothing but the contemplative vision of God, and so far he is saying much what
Aristotle, or his scholar, Eudemus, had said
before him.[83]   But when he proceeds to the
further inference that " the ultimate felicity
of man is not to be had in this present life," [84]
he is saying something quite alien to the spirit
of Aristotle, and, in fact, repeating the burden
of Plato's *Phaedo*.[85]

The conception of human life as a pilgrimage
from exile to our true home which permeates
all the best mediaeval thought about ethics and
religion has, in fact, come from Pythagoras

himself through Plato and the Academy; there is little in it congenial to the temper of Aristotle. If we are to attach any definite meaning to the popular distinction between the naturally Platonist and the naturally Aristotelian types of mind, we might perhaps say that the born Platonists are those who find the world at its best a place of exile, the born Aristotelians those who are by nature "at home" in it. No real Platonist can eliminate eschatology from his religion, however satisfied he may be that all eschatologies are only the imaginative expression of a hope. "He that sat upon the throne said: 'Lo, I am making all things new.'" "We are awaiting new heavens and a new earth, according to his promise, where righteousness is at home." [86] It is not likely that the writers of these passages were under any Platonic influences, but you may rest assured that if the words send no thrill through you, you are not among the *animae naturaliter Platonicae*. It may not be altogether idle to ask the speculative question what would have been the response of the great minds of antiquity to the Gospel, if it had been proclaimed to them. Aristotle, one feels fairly sure, would have been wholly un-

moved by a message from " barbarians " un-
versed alike in logic, in cosmology and in
biology. The most favourable reaction would
pretty certainly have come from Plato and the
great Platonizing poet, Virgil; perhaps we
might add Cicero, if one could be a little more
sure that the Roman magistrate and lawyer in
him would not have overpowered the Platonist.

This little book much reach its period here.
It would have been pleasant to speak of the
direct influence of Plato's natural theology on
Cudworth and the rest of a goodly succession
of divines of our own speech from the Restoration to the present day, if our space would
have allowed. Still pleasanter would it have
been to trace the influence of the poet in Plato,
as distinct from the man of science, on the
great poetic literature of the later world,
through Virgil, Dante, Chaucer and many
another, down to singers who are still
with us. But that is a topic which we
have reluctantly had to exclude almost wholly
from our purview. In truth, the story of all
that our living civilization owes to Plato could
only be told adequately in a complete history
of the thought and literature of the Western
world from his day to ours. These few frag-

mentary and imperfect pages will have done all they were intended to do if they provoke a reader's interest sufficiently to lead him on to serious and connected study, for himself, of the man of whom Aristotle wrote that the bad should not be allowed even to praise him.

NOTES AND BIBLIOGRAPHY

NOTES

1. Plato, *Ep.*, VII. 341. b–d.

2. Cicero, *Academica Priora*, 13: Antiochi magister Philo, magnus vir . . . negat . . . duas esse Academias, erroremque eorum qui ita putarunt coarguit.

3. Plato, *Rep.*, VI. 509 b. 8–10: "Though the Good is not Being but actually on the other side of Being, which it surpasses in dignity and power."

4. Augustine, *Confessiones*, VII. 9. 14; sed quia Verbum caro factum est et habitavit in nobis, non ibi legi.

5. For the mediaeval view of Boethius, see Dante, *Paradiso*, X. 128: "da martiro E da essilio venne a questa pace," and for the effect of the study of the *Consolatio* on Dante himself, *Convivio*, II. 12. 2: "misimi a leggere quello non conosciuto da molti libro di Boezio, nel quale, cattivo e discacciato, consolato s'avea."

6. St. Thomas treats them as an unquestionable authority. So Dante (*Paradiso*, X. 116) says that "Dionysius" "più a dentro vide L'angelica natura e'l ministero."

7. Étienne Gilson, *La Philosophie au moyen Âge*, I. 118–126. Among the "new" translators were St. Thomas' friend William of Morbeke and Robert Grosseteste, who translated the *Ethics*.

8. Étienne Gilson, *La Philosophie au moyen Âge*, II. 1–35; *Études de Philosophie Médiévale*, 77–124.

9. Étienne Gilson, *La Philosophie au moyen Âge*, II. 46: "Oxford, où vont affluer les sciences nouvelles empruntées aux Arabes, recueillera et fera fructifier l'héritage de Chartres; on y restera fidèle au platonisme augustinien, on y saura les langues et l'on y enseignera les mathématiques dont Paris se désintéressera."

10. É. Gilson *op. cit.*, II. 153: "Il faut donc reléguer dans le domaine des légendes l'histoire d'une Renaissance

de la pensée succédant à des siècles de sommeil, d'obscurité et d'erreurs. La philosophie moderne n'a pas eu de lutte à soutenir pour conquérir les ·droits de la raison contre le moyen âge; c'est au contraire le moyen âge qui les a conquis pour elle, et l'acte même par lequel le XVIIe siècle s'imaginait abolir l'oeuvre des siècles précédents ne faisait que le. continuer."

11. É. Gilson, *Études de Philosophie Médiévale,* 146 ff.

12. A. N. Whitehead, *The Concept of Nature,* 17–18.

13. Plato, *Timaeus,* 51 d–e.

14. Plato, *Theaetetus,* 185–186.

15. Cf. Lotze, *Logic,* Bk. III. chapter 4 (English translation Vol. II. 200–222).

16. Plato, *Timaeus,* 27 d 4–29 b2.

17. Plato, *Timaeus,* 29 c7: "If our account prove no less likely than another, we should be satisfied, remembering ' that I who speak and you who are to judge of what I say are but men, and so it becomes us to be satisfied with the likely story about such things and to look for nothing more.'" *Op. cit.,* 48 d: "I shall keep in mind what we spoke of at first, the character of a likely story, and do my best to tell a story about each and all of these matters no less but more likely than that which we gave at first."

18. Plato, *Republic,* V. 479 a, *Phaedo,* 73–74.

19. Aristotle, *Metaphysics,* A 987 b11–12; Plato, *Phaedo,* 100 d, *Parmenides,* 130 b.

20. Plato, *Phaedo,* 76 c–d, *Timaeus,* 43 a–44 c.

21. The full development of the illustration is given in *Meno,* 82 b–83 e, 84 d–85 b.

22. Plato, *Phaedo,* 100 a3–101 e.

23. Plato, *Republic,* VI. 510 b2–511 d5, VII. 533 b1–e 2.

24. It is an indication of the same thing that the only propositions in Euclid's *Elements* which are provided with "analyses" are XIII. 1–5, the fundamental propositions of the section which treats of the inscription of the "figures of Plato," — the regular solids — in the sphere.

25. See particularly Plato, *Parmenides,* 130 b–d, where Socrates is sure that there are Forms of "the just," "the

fine," "the good," not quite so sure about Forms of "man," "fire," "water," and inclined to think that there are no Forms of things like "hair," "mud," "dirt." And observe that the Pythagorean Timaeus never refers, in the ethical part of his discourse, to Forms at all.

26. It is indeed admitted by the orthodox tradition generally that angels and saints in Heaven see God *per essentiam suam*, though never fully and completely, but this vision is "supernatural," a gift of "grace," (Thomas, *Summa, c. Gent.*, III. 52–53). Whether the "vision" is ever bestowed in this life was a disputed point. The Thomist view is that if vouchsafed at all, it is only vouchsafed in an exceptional condition of *raptus* or "ecstacy" to a few chosen persons.

27. *Romans*, I. 20. Cf., e.g., Bonaventura *Itinerarium Mentis in Deum*, II. 13, where the text is quoted to show that *qui nolunt ista advertere et Deum in his omnibus cognoscere, benedicere et amare inexcusabiles sunt;* Thomas, *Summa, c. Gent.*, I. 12, where it is made an argument against the view that the existence of God "cannot be discovered by reason, but is held only by the way of faith and revelation."

28. On the "divine language" see Berkeley, *Alciphron*, Dialogue IV. 7–12; *New Theory of Vision*, §§ 143–148.

28a. *Republic*, VI. 508–9.

29. Dante (*Paradiso*, XXIV. 130–141) called upon by St. Peter to show that he possesses saving faith, replies by a simple profession of his belief in the doctrine of the Trinity.

30. See Malebranche, *Entretiens Metaphysiques*, I. 6: "vôtre chambre n'est point visible. Ce n'est point proprement vôtre chambre que ie voy, lorsque ie la regarde: puisque ie pourrois bien voir tout ce que ie voy maintenant, quand même Dieu l'auroit détruite. Les dimensions que ie voy sont immuables, éternelles, necessaires."

31. Cf. Leibniz, *Nouveaux Essais*, I. 1. 1: "je crois même que toutes les pensées et actions de notre âme viennent de son propre fond, sans pouvoir lui être données par les sens;" II. 1. 1: "les objets externes sensibles

ne sont que *médiates* parcequ'ils ne sauroient agir im-médiatement sur l' âme. Dieu seul est l'objet externe immédiat."

32. For Thomas Reid's version of the doctrine see *Essays on The Intellectual Powers of Man,* Essay II, " Of the Powers we have by means of our external senses," Chapters 7-16, Edinburgh, 1812. It is noteworthy that in Essay VI, *" Of Judgment,"* Chapter 3, Reid ex-pressly says of the Platonic theory of knowledge that " when it is purged " of its " extravagant " part, (by which he means the treatment of Forms as " things," which has no real foundation in Plato), " I apprehend it to be the only intelligible and rational system concerning ideas."

33. The remark will apply not only to the influence of Weierstrass and his followers on the Calculus, the theory of Functions and the doctrine of the " irrational " generally, but to the creation of an arithmetic of infinites by Cantor and to such an attempt at a rigidly philosoph-ical geometry as is made in Grassmann's *Ausdehnungs-lehre.* The question, suggested by Grassmann's work, whether geometry is not rather a parallel development to arithmetic than an application of it, arises at once when we attempt to interpret the Aristotelian notices of the Academic doctrine of " magnitudes."

34. We may note, besides the advocacy of a " return to the *Timaeus"* by Professor Whitehead, the marked influence of the same work on M. Meyerson's important book *L'Explication dans les Sciences,* Paris, 1921, which bears a motto from the dialogue on its title page.

35. *Philebus,* 11, d 5.

36. *Republic,* IX. 583b–588a; *Philebus,* 44–50.

37. *Gorgias,* 467.

38. For all this see the exposition at *Laws,* V. 726–732d.

39. *Laws,* V. 732e–734e.

40. For this criticism see particularly *Republic,* VIII. 557a–558c, where the bitterness of tone is presumably to be explained by the fact that the speaker is Socrates, who had, as a young man, seen all the splendid promise of the Periclean era, and in later life learned by hard experience

what Periclean democracy without a Pericles meant. Plato's own estimate of the possibilities of "democracy," safeguarded by a fundamental "law of the constitution," is given in *Politicus*, 303a–b, and is much more discriminating. In *Laws*, III. 693d ff., he argues for a combination of the "monarchical" and "democratic" elements as the most satisfactory practical constitution.

41. That the views about the place of women in society advocated in the fifth book of the *Republic* are actually those of Socrates is proved by the extant fragments of the *Aspasia* of Aeschines of Sphettus. See John Burnet, "Socrates," in Hastings' *Encyclopaedia of Religion and Ethics*, Vol. XI. We can see from the *Laws* that Plato fully believed in the principle. Aristotle held, on the contrary, that a woman is a naturally inferior being, and that what is virtuous in her would be faulty in a man. "Modesty — or courage or justice — is not the same thing in a woman as in a man, as Socrates fancied it was. . . . As the poet says of woman . . . 'silence in a woman is gracious,' but this does not hold of a man," *Politics*, I. 1260a 21 ff; "a man would be thought a coward if he were brave in the fashion of a brave woman, and a woman forward if she were modest in the degree proper to the good man," *ib.*, III. 1277b 21.

42. For excellent comments on the political "morality" of the Romans in the period when the Republic began consciously to aim at *Weltmacht* see E. A. Freeman, *History of Federal Government in Greece and Italy*,[2] London, 1893, ed. by J. B. Bury, chapter ix. §§ 1–2; C. Thirlwall, *History of Greece*, London, 1835, chapter lxvi. Corneille's *Nicomède* is a fine literary presentation of the theme.

43. For the events at Sparta here referred to see Plutarch's *Lives* of Agis and Cleomenes, Thirlwall, *History of Greece*, c's. LXII, LXIV, and for Demetrius at Athens Plutarch's *Life* of Demetrius, Thirlwall, *op. cit.*, c.LIX.

44. *Laws*, III. 676–681e (prehistoric days), 682a–683c (Trojan war and its sequel), 683c–693c (the Peloponnesian kingdoms), 693d–701e (Persia and Athens).

45. As Prof. C. C. J. Webb has said, "personality" has come into Ethics as a technical term from Theology, particularly from the controversies about the Trinity and the union of the divine and human in Christ, (*God and Personality*, Aberdeen, 1919, Lecture I.). The formula of Boethius *persona est naturae rationabilis individua substantia*, the standard definition of the concept, is directly aimed against the two heretical Christologies of Nestorius and Eutyches.

46. *Republic*, III. 416–417b.

47. The reason for prohibiting family life to the servants of the State is indicated by the remark of R. L. Nettleship that Plato is alive to the dangers of "nepotism." The *père de famille* will always be tempted to use his official position for the benefit of his personal connections.

48. The estates are thus perpetual freeholds, and it is demanded that they shall be as nearly as possible of equal value. The community of the *Laws* is not a "proletariat" but a society of "peasant farmers." Collectivism is an ideal of town-dwelling "industrials," a class which the *Laws* does not recognize. The prohibition of "common cultivation" (*Laws*, 739e 8) is clearly meant to prevent the careless and idle from benefiting by the industry of their neighbours; they are not to participate in an "increment" which, as regards them, is unearned. Plato therefore contemplates differences in "personal" property between his citizens, though he proposes to keep them within bounds by a hundred per cent Income Tax on all personal property beyond a fixed limit.

49. *Laws*, IV. 715 e 7–716 b 5. For the figure of the puppet-show see *Laws*, I. 644d7–645b1, VII. 803c–804b.

50. Contemporary Thomism is, in many of its representatives, more cut-and-dried than St. Thomas's own thought. Cf. *Summa Theolog.*, II^a II^{ae}, *Quaest.* 2, Art. 7. *ad fin.*

51. *Summa c. Gent.*, IV. 70: Omne peccatum ex quadam ignorantia contingit . . . Tunc igitur solum homo securus potest esse a peccato secundum voluntatem quando

secundum intellectum securus est ab ignorantia et errore. III. 71: Impossibile est ut agens operetur aliquod malum, nisi propter hoc quod intendit aliquid bonum.

52. *Op. cit.*, III. 110: In diabolo peccatum fuit in hoc quod proprium bonum non rettulit ad divinum bonum.

53. Cf. the volume on *The Greek Fathers,* in this Series.

54. The lowering of tone is ultimately due to that exaggerated estimate of the life of scientific research which leads Aristotle to deny that there is anything in God at all corresponding to " moral " virtue. Morality is thus cut loose from religion, and by inevitable consequence becomes a matter of secondary, though still high, importance for humanity. The unfortunate one-sidedness which arises from this comparative neglect of ethics as one of the foundations of religion naturally tends to make the distinctions between " nature " and " grace," " reason " and " revelation " unduly rigid. The results of the mischief are seen markedly outside the limits of " Thomism." Pascal meant to be an Augustinian, but contrast the views of the gentile philosophic morality which colour his *Pensées* with those of the *de Civitate Dei!*

55. But possibly he would have escaped by incurring an earlier sentence of banishment from Plato's city by his grossly licentious comedy of the *Candelaio.*

56. The differences are that, for want of a firm grasp of the principle that *quidquid petitur petitur sub specie boni,* Butler makes " interest " an " active principle " distinct from others and so involves himself in the difficulty about a possible conflict of duty with interest, and that he treats " resentment " as a mere " particular passion " on the level of hunger, or sexual appetite, or the passion for high play. Here his psychology seems inferior to Plato's.

57. See the *De regimine principum* of Thomas, or, for a more commonplace treatment, the *Eruditio regum et principum* written by Gilbert of Tournai for St. Louis. Dante's *Monarchia* exhibits the Thomist theory coloured by the author's strong personal convictions of the need of

[141]

a single world-ruler. He looks to the "Emperor" for the same services which a modern enthusiast expects from a "League of Nations." His theory that the Empire belongs directly and "of divine right" to the "Roman people" seems to be peculiar to himself.

58. For the connection of the 17th century theories of the "social contract" with Roman Law see the admirable exposition in O. F. Gierke, *Political Theories of the Middle Age*, translated by F. W. Maitland, Cambridge, 1900, and for the connection of the Academy with Hellenistic Law cf. John Burnet, *Greek Philosophy, Pt. I.*, London, 1914, pp. 303–304.

59. On Varro's classification see Augustine, *De Civitate Dei*, VI. 5–7. For the remark of Q. Mucius Scaevola, the Pontifex, see *op. cit.*, IV. 27, with Augustine's comments. Hobbes's saying that "religion is not philosophy but law" is exactly in the Roman spirit.

60. The argument is given at length in *Laws*, X. 891b8–899d2, with which compare *Phaedrus*, 245c5–246c2. The second of the three heresies is refuted, *Laws*, X. 899d 4–905d 1, and the third, *Laws*, X. 905d 8–907b 4.

61. On this point see *Laws*, X. 888e 4 ff.

62. *Laws*, X. 896e4, where it is a pure blunder to find any hint of an "evil world-soul." Plato only means that, since there is disorder as well as order, in the world, the "best soul" cannot be the only one. All through the argument we must understand by the "orderliness" of a motion not only its "regularity" but the beneficial results it produces. In the end the "orderly" motions mean those which further the growth and preservation of spiritual civilization, not simply those which are mathematically "uniform."

63. In *Ep.*, XIII. 363b5, Plato tells Dionysius II that he will distinguish letters which are really urgent from those which he has to write as a mere matter of politeness by speaking of God in the opening salutations of the first, of "gods" in those of the others.

64. For the workings of this law see *Laws*, X. 903e 3–905d 1. The conclusion of the whole matter is that

" you shall assuredly never be passed over by God's judgement, not though you make yourself never so small and hide in the depths of the earth, nor exalt yourself to heaven; you must pay the due penalty, either while you are still among us, or, after your passage hence, in Hades, or, it may be, by removal to some still wilder region," *op. cit.,* 905a 4 ff.

65. Only that, speaking strictly, Plato's third tenet should be *called* " accountability " rather than " freedom." But this is a mere matter of words, since on Kant's view it is precisely and only because we are accountable that we have the right to assert that we are free. (There is no mysterious immediate revelation of freedom in Kant's theory.)

66. For a further account of the history of the " proofs of the existence of God " from Plato to Kant the present writer may be allowed to refer to his article *Theism* in Hastings' *Encyclopaedia of Religion and Ethics,* Vol. XII, where references will be found to the literature of the subject.

67. As to Anaxagoras see John Burnet, *Early Greek Philosophy,*[3] London, pp. 251–257 and the present writer's article, " On the Date of the Trial of Anaxagoras," in *The Classical Quarterly,* XI. 81–87 (1917). As to Socrates, see Burnet, *Greek Philosophy, Pt. I.* chapter 10.

68. For the laws against heresy see *Laws,* X. 907d4–909d2. The reason why the worst class of heretics escape the death penalty is that their lifelong imprisonment itself prevents them from doing further mischief, and death is not to be inflicted superfluously.

69. It is hard to accept the view suggested in C. Ritter's *Commentary* on the *Laws* that an offender who has completed his term of imprisonment is expected to make a formal " abjuration " and that refusal to do so is followed by death. I understand Plato to mean that a first offence is " purged " by the imprisonment, and that death is the penalty for a second conviction.

70. Innocent's theory was embodied in legislation by the Emperor Frederic II, in the Constitution promulgated

for the Empire in 1220, and that promulgated for Lombardy in 1224. This is how "stake and faggot" came to be the regular penalty for contumacious heresy. (*Encyc. Religion and Ethics,* art. *Inquisition,* Vol. VII.)

71. For all this see Aristotle, *Metaphysics,* Λ 1072a19–1073a13, 1074a14–1075a11.

72. Aristotle, *Ethics,* X. 1178b7–23.

73. Cf., in particular, *Ethics,* X. 1178a9–23.

74. By a synod held at Constantinople under Justinian in 543, but the oecumenical authority of this body is very doubtful.

75. Aristotle, *de Anima, B.* 413a9, where the question is mooted whether the soul is to the body as "the sailor to the vessel." In the thirteenth century the words were regarded as an authentic account of Plato's psychology. Cf. *Summa c. Gent.,* II. 57 Plato . . . dicens animam esse in corpore sicut nauta est in navi.

76. *Summa c. Gent.,* I. 13, where the proofs are given very fully with references to the Aristotelian text.

77. *Op. cit.,* I. 49.

78. *Summa c. Gent.,* I. 93, *quod in Deo virtutes sunt quae sunt circa actiones.*

79. Brevity makes it necessary to speak here very much "in the rough." The point of contrast is that, like Berkeley, or, in a rather different way, Whitehead, Plato builds up the physical world without "matter," Aristotle introduces "matter," though in the dubiously tenable form of a "potentiality" which is *actually* nothing.

80. Dante (*Inferno,* III. 8.) speaks of certain things which, like Hell, are "eternal" creations. The things meant are "first matter," the angels, and the "heavens." The Aristotelian doctrine is that only what is compounded of "matter" and "form" is perishable, since "perishing" means the transition of the same matter into a fresh form. The angels are imperishable because they are "separate forms" with no "matter," "first matter" because it is "matter" with no "form," the "heavens" because their "matter" is combined with a "form" which completely

realizes all the inherent potentialities of the "matter," and so no room is left for "development." This is precisely the teaching of the *Summa c. Gent.*

81. *Summa c. Gent.,* III. 74: *Quanto aliqua causa est superior causato, tanto est maioris virtutis, unde eius causalitas ad plura se extendit.*

82. *Summa Theologiae,* I^a, *Quaest.* 46, Art. 1.

83. *Ethica Eudemia,* Θ 1249b16: "What choice, then, or possession of the natural goods . . . will most produce the contemplation of God, that choice or possession is best; this is the noblest standard, but . . . any that through deficiency or excess hinders one from the contemplation and service of God is bad." For a powerful defence of the genuineness of the *E.E.,* see Jaeger, *Aristoteles,* Berlin, 1925, pp. 236–270.

84. *Summa c. Gent.,* III. 48: *quod ultima felicitas hominis non sit in hac vita.* It is only right to say that Aristotle has taught the doctrine as emphatically as Plato or Thomas in his dialogue *Eudemus,* written in or soon after 354 B.C., during Plato's life-time. But it disappears from his matured thought as expressed in the *Nicomachean Ethics.* Jaeger (*op. cit.*) has made it very probable that the *Eudemian Ethics* and the passages about the "imperishable" active intellect in the third book of the *de Anima* represent a transitional stage in Aristotle's mental development.

85. *Phaedo,* 68b, the "lover of wisdom" will welcome death when it comes in God's good time, because he is so certain that "he will never find wisdom in its purity anywhere but in yonder world."

86. *Apoc.,* XXI. 5; II. *Pet.,* III. 13.

BIBLIOGRAPHY

[The bibliography has been made as brief as possible.
Only a few quite indispensable works are mentioned, for
the most part in the English language.]

PLATO, *Works.* The most recent and satisfactory edition
of the whole text is that of John Burnet, *Platonis
Opera* in the *Scriptorum Classicorum Bibliotheca
Oxoniensis,* 5 vols., 1899–1906. A critical text of the
complete works, accompanied by French translation,
is in course of publication at Paris (société d'édition
"*Les Belles Lettres*"), vol. 1, 1920, vol. 2, 1921,
vol. 3, part 1, 1923, part 2, 1924, vol. 8, part 1, 1923,
part 2, 1924. The completest English translation
is that of Benjamin Jowett, 4 vols., Oxford, 1871,
which unfortunately does not include *Epinomis,
Epistles,* nor most of the Platonic "apocrypha,"
and stands also in need of careful revision. There
is a useful complete translation into German by
O. Apelt and others, included in the *Philosophische
Bibliothek* published by F. Meiner of Leipzig. In
the *Golden Treasury Series* (Macmillan) are contained three useful volumes, the *Republic* (tr., Davies
and Vaughan), *Trial and Death of Socrates* (*Euthy-
phro, Apology, Crito, Phaedo,* tr., F. J. Church), *The
Phaedrus, Lysis* and *Protagoras of Plato* (tr., J.
Wright). H. N. Fowler, *Plato, with an English Translation,* in *The Loeb Classical Library;* 2 vols. have
appeared. London and New York, 1921.

ADAM, JAMES, *The Vitality of Platonism.* Cambridge,
England, 1911.
BARKER, E., *The Greek Political Theory: Plato and his
Predecessors.* London, 1918. (N.B. This is a much
enlarged edition of the older book.)

[146]

BIBLIOGRAPHY

BURNET, JOHN, *Greek Philosophy, Part I, Thales to Plato.*
London and New York, 1914.

BURNET, J., *Shakespeare and Greek Philosophy*, in *Book of homage to Shakespeare* (ed., I. Gollancz). Oxford, 1916.

BURNET, J., Articles, " Pythagoras," " Socrates," in James Hastings' *Encyclopaedia of Religion and Ethics.* 12 vols. Edinburgh and New York, 1908–21.

GILSON, É., *La Philosophie au moyen Âge.* 2 vols. Collection Payot, Paris, 1922.

GILSON, É., *Le Thomisme.*[2] Paris, 1923.

GILSON, É., *Études de Philosophie Médiévale.* Strasbourg, (*Publications de l'Université*) 1921.

HARRISON, J. S., *Platonism in English Poetry* of the 16th. and 17th. Centuries. New York, 1903. [G. D. H.]

HÜGEL, BARON F. VON., *Eternal Life.* Edinburgh, 1912.

INGE, W. R., *The Philosophy of Plotinus.* 2 vols. London and New York, 1918.

INGE, W. R., " Ruskin and Plato," in *Ruskin the Prophet* (Ed. by J. H. Whitehouse). London and New York, 1921. [G. D. H.]

JAEGER, W., *Aristoteles.* Berlin, 1925.

MILHAUD, G., *Les Philosophes-Géomètres de la Grèce.* Paris, 1900.

MORE, PAUL E., *The Religion of Plato.* Princeton, 1921.

NETTLESHIP, R. L., *Lectures on the " Republic " of Plato.* London, 1897. (Vol. 2 of *Philosophical Lectures and Remains of Richard Lewis Nettleship,* London, 1897.)

RITCHIE, D. G., *Plato*, in " The World's Epoch Makers " Series. Edinburgh, 1902.

RITTER, C., *Platon, Sein Leben, Seine Schriften, Seine Lehre.* 2 vols. Munich, 1910, 1923.

RITTER, C., *Platon. Gesetze. Kommentar.* Leipzig, 1896.

RITTER, C., *Platons Staat: Darstellung des Inhalts.* Stuttgart, 1909.

ROBIN, L., *La Théorie Platonicienne des Idées et des Nombrés.* Paris, 1908.

ROBIN, L., *Études sur la signification et la place de la Physique dans la Philosophie de Platon.* Paris, 1919.

[147]

BIBLIOGRAPHY

ROBIN, L., *La Pensée grecque et les origines de l'Esprit scientifique.* Paris, 1923.

ROSS, W. D., *Aristotle.* London, 1923.

SHOREY, PAUL, " The Unity of Plato's Thought," in *The Decennial Publications of the University of Chicago.* pp. 129–214. Chicago, 1904.

STEWART, J. A., *Plato's Doctrine of Ideas.* Oxford, 1909.

STEWART, J. A., *The Myths of Plato.* London and New York, 1905.

STEWART, J. A., " Platonism in English Poetry," in G. S. Gordon's *English Literature and the Classics.* Oxford, 1912.

TAYLOR, A. E., *Plato,* in the " Philosophies Ancient and Modern " Series. London and New York, 1911.

TAYLOR, A. E., *Aristotle*[2]. London and Edinburgh, 1919.

WENLEY, R. M., *The Affinity of Plato's Republic for Modern Thought.* Berkeley, California, 1905. [G. D. H.]

WHITEHEAD, A. N., *The Concept of Nature.* Cambridge, England, 1920.

WHITTAKER, T., *The Neo-Platonists.*[2] Cambridge, England, 1918.

WICKSTEED, P. H., *The Reactions between Dogma and Philosophy illustrated from the Works of S. Thomas Aquinas.* London, 1920.

A few editions with English commentaries should be mentioned:

The *Apology,* Ed., J. Riddell. Oxford, 1867.

The *Phaedo,* Ed., J. Burnet. Oxford, 1911.

The *Republic,* Ed., J. Adam. 2 vols. Cambridge, England, 1902.

The *Republic,* Eds., B. Jowett and L. Campbell. Oxford, 1894.

The *Theaetetus,* Ed., L. Campbell. Oxford, 1883.[2]

The *Sophistes and Politicus,* Ed., L. Campbell. Oxford, 1867.

The *Laws,* Ed., E. B. England. 2 vols. Manchester, 1921.

[148]

INDEX OF PROPER NAMES

INDEX OF PROPER NAMES

ABELARD, P., 21
Albert (the Great), 22, 23, 47, 50, 118
Albert (of Saxony), 24
Alexander of Aphrodisias, 15, 121
Alfred (King), 19
Ambrose St., 18, 84
Anaxagoras, 109
Anselm St., 45, 52, 108
Antiochus of Ascalon, 9, 10
Arcesilaus, 7, 8
Aristotle, 4, 5, 7, 14–16, 21 ff., 57 ff., 67, 68, 71, 75, 82–87, 109, 113 ff., 130, 139, 141, 144, 145
Atticus, 11

Augustine St., Augustinianism, 18, 26, 42, 46 ff., 58 ff., 80, 82, 84 ff., 95, 127, 142

Averroes, 121

BACON (FRANCIS), 26
Bacon (Roger), 23, 50
Barrow, Isaac, 27
Basil St., 84
Berkeley, 46, 53, 54, 144
Boethius, 18, 19, 84 ff., 135
Bonaventura St., 23, 47
Bruno, Giordano, 25, 85
Buridan, John, 24
Butler, 27, 58, 63, 86

CAMPANELLA, 25, 90
Carneades, 8
Cavalieri, 27
Chalcidius, 20
Chaucer, 19, 131
Clarke, S., 86, 87
Clement (of Alexandria), 17
Crantor, 7, 9
Cudworth, 26, 86, 87, 131

DANTE, 19, 28, 131, 135, 137, 142, 144
Democritus, 7
Descartes, 25, 36, 51 ff., 108, 122
"Dionysius," 19, 122

ERIGENA, JOANNES SCOTUS, 18, 20, 95
Euclid, 136
Eudemus, 129
Eudoxus, 40

FREDERIC II., 144

GALILEO, 24–25, 111
Gilson, É., 22–23, 135–136
Green, T. H., 87
Gregory (the Great), St., 94
Gregory (of Nyssa), 18, 84, 95
Grosseteste, R., 23
Grote, J., 27

[151]

INDEX OF PROPER NAMES

HILARY ST., 42
Hipparchus, 15
Hobbes, 86, 88, 142
Honorius (of Autun), 21
Hooker, R., 26, 88
Hugh of St. Victor, 21
Hume, D., 52, 55
Hutcheson, Fr., 86

INNOCENT III, 22, 112, 144

JULIAN, 13
Justinian, 6, 14

KANT, 29, 41, 49, 56 ff., 58, 59, 82, 107 ff., 143
Kepler, 24

LEIBNIZ, 27, 29, 53 ff., 108, 137
Locke, 88

MACROBIUS, 20
Malebranche, 53, 137
Marlowe, 26
Maximus (of Tyre), 8
Medici, Lorenzo d., 25
Meyerson, É., 138
More, H., 27, 86
More, Sir T., 90

NEWTON, 27
Nicholas (of Autrecour), 24

OCKHAM, William of, 24
Origen, 17, 95, 119

PANAETIUS, 9
Pascal, 59
Paul St., 45
Philo (of Alexandria), 10, 84

Philo (of Larissa), 9
Plotinus, 11–13, 15, 16, 42
Plutarch, 8, 9, 11, 139
Porphyry, 11, 13, 16
Posidonius, 9, 10
Price, R., 27, 87
Proclus, 13, 14, 19, 83, 122, 124
Pythagoras,　⎰ 4, 35, 42,
Pythagoreanism,⎱ 93, 97, 129

RABELAIS, 28
Reid, 55, 138
Ritter, C., 143
Rousseau, 88
Ruskin, 91

SCAEVOLA, Q. MUCIUS, 98, 142
Shaftesbury, 86
Shakespeare, 26
Shelley, 91, 116
Simplicius, 16
Smith, J., 86
Socrates, 4, 35–38, 41, 47, 61, 67, 81, 97, 103, 109, 138
Spinoza, 58

THEOPHRASTUS, 15

Thomas Aquinas St.,
Thomism,
⎧ 22 ff., 42,
⎪ 45, 47 ff.,
⎪ 79 ff., 82–
⎨ 84,
⎪ 88, 108 ff.,
⎪ 118 ff., 137,
⎩ 141, 145

VARRO, M. TERENTIUS, 97–98

INDEX OF PROPER NAMES

Virgil, 94, 131

WALLIS, 27
Webb, C. C. J., 140
Wells, H. G., 90

Whitehead, A. N., 27, 138, 144

XENOCRATES, 7, 9

ZENO (THE STOIC), 9

Our Debt to Greece and Rome

AUTHORS AND TITLES

HOMER. *John A. Scott.*

SAPPHO. *David M. Robinson.*

EURIPIDES. *F. L. Lucas.*

ARISTOPHANES. *Louis E. Lord.*

DEMOSTHENES. *Charles D. Adams.*

THE POETICS OF ARISTOTLE. *Lane Cooper.*

GREEK RHETORIC AND LITERARY CRITICISM. *W. Rhys Roberts.*

LUCIAN. *Francis G. Allinson.*

CICERO AND HIS INFLUENCE. *John C. Rolfe.*

CATULLUS. *Karl P. Harrington.*

LUCRETIUS AND HIS INFLUENCE. *George Depue Hadzsits.*

OVID. *Edward Kennard Rand.*

HORACE. *Grant Showerman.*

VIRGIL. *John William Mackail.*

SENECA THE PHILOSOPHER. *Richard Mott Gummere.*

APULEIUS. *Elizabeth Hazelton Haight.*

MARTIAL. *Paul Nixon.*

PLATONISM. *Alfred Edward Taylor.*

ARISTOTELIANISM. *John L. Stocks.*

STOICISM. *Robert Mark Wenley.*

LANGUAGE AND PHILOLOGY. *Roland G. Kent.*

AUTHORS AND TITLES

AESCHYLUS AND SOPHOCLES.   *J. T. Sheppard.*

GREEK RELIGION.   *Walter Woodburn Hyde.*

SURVIVALS OF ROMAN RELIGION.   *Gordon J. Laing.*

MYTHOLOGY.   *Jane Ellen Harrison.*

ANCIENT BELIEFS IN THE IMMORTALITY OF THE SOUL.   *Clifford H. Moore.*

STAGE ANTIQUITIES.   *James Turney Allen.*

PLAUTUS AND TERENCE.   *Gilbert Norwood.*

ROMAN POLITICS.   *Frank Frost Abbott.*

PSYCHOLOGY, ANCIENT AND MODERN.   *G. S. Brett.*

ANCIENT AND MODERN ROME.   *Rodolfo Lanciani.*

WARFARE BY LAND AND SEA.   *Eugene S. McCartney.*

THE GREEK FATHERS.   *James Marshall Campbell.*

GREEK BIOLOGY AND MEDICINE.   *Henry Osborn Taylor.*

MATHEMATICS.   *David Eugene Smith.*

LOVE OF NATURE AMONG THE GREEKS AND ROMANS.   *H. R. Fairclough.*

ANCIENT WRITING AND ITS INFLUENCE.   *B. L. Ullman.*

GREEK ART.   *Arthur Fairbanks.*

ARCHITECTURE.   *Alfred M. Brooks.*

ENGINEERING.   *Alexander P. Gest.*

MODERN TRAITS IN OLD GREEK LIFE.   *Charles Burton Gulick.*

ROMAN PRIVATE LIFE.   *Walton Brooks McDaniel.*

GREEK AND ROMAN FOLKLORE.   *William Reginald Halliday.*

ANCIENT EDUCATION.   *J. F. Dobson.*